AUTUMN BULBS

ROD LEEDS

Autumn
Bulbs

Alpine Garden Society

BT BATSFORD

Many thanks to Jane.

First published 2005

© Rod Leeds 2005

The right of Rod Leeds to be identified as Author of this book has been
asserted by him in accordance with the Copyright, Designs and Patents Act
1988.

Volume © B T Batsford 2005

ISBN 0 7134 8962 6

A CIP catalogue record for this book is available from the British Library.

Printed in Singapore

for the publisher
B T Batsford
The Chrysalis Building
Bramley Road
London W10 6SP

www.chrysalisbooks.co.uk

An imprint of **Chrysalis** Books Group plc

Pictures supplied by Plant Images and the author, unless specified otherwise.

CONTENTS

INTRODUCTION

The fresh and pristine appearance of the bulbous flowers in autumn is one of their particular attractions for the gardener. These new flowers contrast with the tired-looking foliage and the waning splendour of summer flowers, which have withstood the heat and droughts as well as the storms of this season. Some bulbs flower nakedly, with the foliage growing in winter or even the following spring. Autumn flowering is an adaptation to their original climate and environment, which is usually very warm and dry in summer, with very few plants, let alone bulbs, flowering. As the days shorten, temperatures drop and any rain is less inclined to evaporate; in the mountains night-time dews also cool the soil: all elements that initiate bulbs into flowering, with pollination still assured from the hordes of insects that abound in early autumn.

In a cool, temperate climate this adaptation to living is unnecessary, but does give people who live in such a climate the chance to enjoy a surprising diversity of flowers in the garden and under glass from late August through to the end of November. For the purposes of this book the rubicon is near the end of August but, as all growers know, the combination of rainfall, temperature and amounts of sunshine can alter the timing of flowering considerably, none more so than for autumn bulbs.

In this book, the term *bulb* will be extended to cover plants that have a storage organ; this may be a bulb, but could equally well be a rhizome, a tuber or a corm. The flowers described are not all from high mountains – in fact some are found in maritime locations, only just above sea level. Many of these plants can be grown with little preparation in the open garden, whereas some will need growing under glass at some stage of the year to ensure the bulbs can lie dormant in a fairly dry state before resuming some form of growth. There is also a small number that will need cultivation in a cool greenhouse where the temperature does not fall below 1°C (34°F), thus preventing damage from frost.

There are a surprising number of genera available, not just the obvious Mediterranean selections, but also bulbs from the southern hemisphere, especially South Africa. Some of these are adaptable enough to withstand the light levels going into reverse and still produce fine flowers in autumn.

Left: *Crocus nudiflorus 'Orla'*

HISTORY

Early scientific books concentrated on the spring and summer flora, with tulips and lilies taking centre stage in illustrations. Commerce in these bulbs took off in the 17th and 18th centuries, with extraordinary prices paid for some species, notably tulips in the Netherlands in the 17th century and, to a lesser extent, in Britain in the 18th century.

The autumn bulbs *Sternbergia clusiana* and *Crocus clusii* (now known as *Crocus serotinus clusii*) were named after Carolus Clusius, who was probably the first European to seriously cultivate bulbous plants. His books, written in the 16th and 17th centuries, chronicle many new introductions including some colchicum, cyclamen and anemone. Also, many books were written on the medicinal use of plants and here we find many descriptions of *Crocus sativus* and the uses of saffron.

In the 18th century botanical expeditions really got underway, often involving years of work away from home. *Crocus tournefortii* commemorates one such journey by the French botanist J P de Tournefort and his team, who travelled around the eastern Mediterranean some 300 years ago. There were numerous explorations, gradually extending further from Europe, introducing thousands of plants to cultivation. Species are still being newly described. In the 1950s, the very distinctive *Crocus goulimyi* was described by Dr W B Turrill. It was named to commemorate the discovery by Dr C N Goulimy of this species in the Peloponnese. A much paler-flowered colony has within the last ten years been given varietal status as *Crocus goulimyi* var. *leucanthus*. This isolated group in the south-eastern prong of the Peloponnese had only been noted in the 1970s and was not fully evaluated until 1994.

Some small autumn-flowering colchicums are quite tricky to identify. This can clearly be seen by the recent regular publication of newly described species. For the amateur there is a need for these descriptions to be shuffled and a usable key produced, with any anomalies cleared. One problem is the lack of leaves at flowering. It is also sometimes difficult to return to the exact location in spring to measure and record often quite small foliage mixed in with the luxuriant herbage of all the annuals and spring-flowering bulbs. It seems that the timing of the flowering of colchicums is very precise each autumn, quite regardless of the rainfall, although the flowers soon fade and then shrivel if the summer drought persists.

Left: *Crocus goulimyi*
Opposite: *Crocus goulimyi* var. *leucanthus*

With the development of less expensive and more frequent air travel the hillsides are being much more extensively searched for new or subtly different forms of well-known species. New roads give easy access to hitherto hidden areas, so it is natural that many new plants, including autumnal ones, are finding their way into our gardens and frames. These introductions are sometimes reintroductions of very special bulbs. From the Pyrenees came *Crocus nudiflorus* 'Orla', named after the nearby Port de Orla, a beautiful albino form found by Joy Hulme.

According to G Maw in his nineteenth-century monograph on crocus, white forms of *Crocus nudiflorus* had been noted, but a hundred years later there were none left in cultivation. Relatively new to cultivation is *Galanthus peshmenii* from south-western Turkey and an adjacent island. This plant was first thought to be a Turkish *Galanthus reginae-olgae* and distributed as such for a few years until further investigation revealed distinct differences, especially when in full leaf. It is proving to be very amenable to cultivation and profligate with its offspring.

There is one downside to this ease of accessibility and the clear defining of sites and that is plant collecting. There are international conventions on the movement of plants and many countries have their own laws to protect their flora. Unfortunately some unscrupulous and anonymous collecting in a wholesale manner has decimated a few sites. It is one thing to collect a little seed, but another to mattock out the plants to fill a sack, with no regard for sustaining the wild population. The collection of many wild species in Turkey for export may seem wrong and indeed may not be sustainable, but it is gradually being subjected to greater regulation with some

attempts to farm the collected stock being developed. These stocks will inevitably require selling at a premium, but this would only represent a tiny fraction of the eventual retail price in Europe. As gardeners, it is usually quite easy to tell a plump, freshly lifted nursery bulb from an often hard, or sometimes even flaccid, bulb that may well have been collected, stored and then subjected to a long journey by road across Europe. In any case, success with these over-dried bulbs has been very low and they rarely represent a bargain.

Once a species is in the garden, the selection of good forms and hybrids really gets underway. The selection and retention of these is initially almost done to contemporary plant fashions and promotions, with those that have something extra surviving to be propagated for generations. In the Netherlands many hybrids from *Colchicum bornmuelleri*, *Colchicum giganteum* and *Colchicum sibthorpii* were selected and named by the firm of Zocher and Co. Mr J J Herbert, as head of the firm, was instrumental in their selection and distribution. Today, a hundred years later, some are still produced, although not by Zocher and Co, which ceased trading in 1930. The ubiquitous *Colchicum* 'Lilac Wonder' is as strong and vibrant as ever and *Colchicum* 'Violet Queen', *Colchicum* 'The Giant', *Colchicum* 'Autumn Queen' and *Colchicum* 'Dandaels' are all very clearly distinct and in cultivation. The cultivars *Colchicum* 'Disraeli' and *Colchicum* 'Premier' are sometimes offered but may have become muddled in the intervening years, as they do not seem to match the old descriptions and paintings.

Left: *Sternbergia lutea* in the Peloponnese, Greece
Below: *Crocus cancellatus mazziaricus*

In Britain during the 19th century the nursery and alpine garden of Backhouse of York were established on a scale unheard of today. An alpine gorge using 400 tons of rock was a showpiece of engineering and a mecca for plants. It was here that one of autumn's most attractive plants was raised, *Colchicum speciosum* 'Album', with its long-lasting white goblets held firmly on pale green tubes. This plant received the Royal Horticultural Society (RHS) First Class Certificate in 1900 and has lived up to this reputation ever since. Mrs R O Backhouse from Sutton Court near Hereford was engaged in breeding and selecting bulbs, notably narcissus and lilies, but also some forms of *Colchicum speciosum*. Two of these – *Colchicum speciosum* 'Huxley' and 'Darwin' – are still in cultivation. The latter is a fairly small, late-flowering selection, which often waits until late October before appearing, whereas *Colchicum speciosum* 'Huxley' is mid-season, with large, overlapping segments of dark purple and of good substance.

Below: *Colchicum speciosum* 'Album' and *Colchicum speciosum* 'Benton End'

In 1996 and 1997 there was an assessment of the large-flowered autumn colchicums by a panel of judges from the RHS for the Award of Garden Merit (AGM). This trial was held at Felbrigg Hall in Norfolk, where one of the UK national collections is held. The trial saw plants grown in near identical conditions of soil and full sunlight in a sheltered garden setting. Repeat visits were made and leaves pressed in spring to aid identification. These awards are a good benchmark to aid selection and are often denoted in nurseries and catalogues by the symbol of a goblet with handles ♈. You can be sure that these plants will thrive in ordinary garden conditions, are widely available and are of particular merit as a decorative garden feature.

From these assessments six selections were awarded the AGM, with a number of others deferred until definite names could be established. In one instance one plant was clearly represented by four different names and it may not be possible to follow the trail back to the oldest and most correct name. In other cases, such as *Colchicum byzantinum* 'Album', a correct epithet was sought because the Latin 'Album' was too late an addition to be retained under the modern naming rules. The appropriate-sounding name *Colchicum byzantinum* 'Innocence' was given to this white plant with small purple tips to each segment. The true or at least agreed naming of historic garden plants is a good service provided by the RHS, as the frustration of buying the same plant under different names is all too common a problem.

Left: *Colchicum speciosum* 'Huxley'

CULTIVATION

Generally, bulbs thrive best in a well-drained soil, which during the dormant period is fairly dry or at least merely moist. This soil is best on the alkaline side of neutral, as most bulbs are found above alkaline rocks such as limestone. There is a large minority of bulbs, however, that are encountered above basic rock formations and these need a slightly different compost, with the addition of some peat or peat substitute.

It is often very informative to read about the habitat where the bulb grows, as often a plant will have colonized only, at a specific aspect or altitude and then be found only in areas where soil has accumulated. Even in potentially very hot countries, cool niches exist where bulbs can thrive in an otherwise inhospitable environment, or they may be found at considerable depth in rocky ground where the bulbs and their ephemeral roots are always cool. In contrast, a few, such as *Urginea maritima*, have very large bulbs and grow with the bulb top visible and exposed to the sun in high summer, without any shade given by the leaves. These few species do need as dry and hot a position as possible in order to flower in higher-latitude gardens.

The majority of these bulbs are dormant in high summer, but not all, so any specific requirements will be given in the A–Z section. Growers will soon be aware that if some of the early-flowering species such as *Leucojum roseum* and *Scilla autumnalis* are grown in pots, then they should be dealt with first when bulb-potting time begins in June.

Right: *Crocus kotschyanus kotschyanus*

Pot cultivation

There are several advantages to growing bulbs in pots, not least of which is the regular handling, which soon gives the grower experience in maintaining and multiplying their stock. Also the proximity of the pots on benches or in frames closer to the eye and nose adds to the enjoyment that can be taken in these attractive plants. As autumn weather becomes more boisterous and wet, the flowers under glass stay in good condition longer. It is also easier to ensure fertilization of those specially favoured plants by dexterity with tweezers, brushes and sharp scissors.

When you acquire your bulbs in late summer, the treatment is similar for the majority. Check the flower stem height and leaf length before deciding on the size of pot. Use plastic or clay pots depending upon your preference; the planting procedure is the same for both, but not the subsequent treatment through the year. Clay pots are slightly porous and by plunging them in sand or a similar product, moisture can be maintained around the roots during the growing season and lessen the range of temperature in the depths of winter and the heights of summer. Plastic pots, on the other hand, especially the square designs, take up less space and can absorb moisture from beneath if the bench is flooded at regular intervals to suit the season. It is not always easy to mix the two types of pot in the same area; they are best segregated and treated accordingly. Whatever your choice, it is always advisable to clean the pot before use to lessen the risk of spreading infection from the previous occupant, and clear out any eggs or even slugs that have taken up residence.

Above: *Crocus hadriaticus*

The drainage hole in the base first needs to be protected against ingress by worms. Worms are fine in the garden but positively damaging in a pot. They become trapped in the compost and turn any beautiful, fluffy, well-drained mix into coagulated mud in no time. If they do get in, it is definitely worth carefully upending the pot and pulling the worms out with a pair of tweezers. A small piece of perforated zinc or aluminium mesh, as used in amateur car bodywork repair, can be fitted over the drainage hole before the compost is added. This will keep out all but the smallest worms, but will not impede drainage.

Some gardeners have their own special mix of compost, but most rely on the John Innes formula of potting composts, which are soil-based and include fertilizers. Mix an equal volume of 4–5mm angular grit with John Innes compost No. 2. This will provide a strong and well-drained medium for growth. These proprietary composts should be very similar, but the grower will soon find that some brands are better than others and it is worth experimenting and asking around to find one that is consistent and accurately mixed. A garden-made compost for bulbs can be mixed, made of one part 4–5mm grit, one part finely sieved and, ideally, sterilized soil and one of leaf mould or sphagnum peat. The volume of grit may need to be increased depending upon the consistency of the soil used. When a pot is filled with compost and then watered, the water must run through immediately; if this does not happen, increase the grit content. When you are satisfied with the drainage, mix in the appropriate amount of John Innes base fertilizer.

The planting of the bulbs can now be considered. Generally they need planting with the same depth of compost above the bulb as the bulb is deep. In the garden this can be increased, as there is ample opportunity for root development, but in a pot following the old adage of twice the depth will leave very little compost for the roots to explore. Some growers spread a shallow layer of sharp sand on the compost and bed the bulb into this strata. I do not believe it facilitates drainage, but it does help with locating the bulbs, particularly small ones at repotting time, and also indicates if the roots have moved the bulb deeper in the pot, thereby indicating the need for a deeper pot next time. For many bulbs it is not necessary to repot every summer, but

you will need to inspect the stock by removing the grit and compost above the bulbs. This is made easier by the guiding layer of sharp sand as the pot is lying on its side and the bulbs either exposed or removed. The bulbs are then replanted or simply top-dressed with the usual compost, to which a little extra bone meal or similar fertilizer has been added.

Once the bulbs are planted the surface of the compost should be covered with about 1cm (½in) of grit. This has many uses, not least of which is the aesthetic. Choose a top dressing that is appropriate – for instance, granite for an acid lover and limestone for the opposite. Crushed flint is a very suitable dressing for many, being virtually dust-free and available in various dimensions to suit the size of the pot and plant. Woodland bulbs are often best top-dressed with a fine bark. Eventually this will rot down into the compost but is easily topped up. A layer of grit protects the leaves and flowers from being splashed when being hand-watered or from heavy rain, and probably slows evaporation from the underlying compost on very hot days. Unfortunately, it does not, as often quoted, protect the plants from marauding molluscs, however sharp and angular, but it does decrease the growth of moss and liverwort within the pot. If, eventually, moss and liverwort do grow, their removal is quite easy as the top layer is so loose. There is a disadvantage in not being able to see the compost and so judge when to water, but experience soon lets you know the frequency required.

Once the bulbs have been set into the pots they need immediate watering and placing in a frame or on a greenhouse bench. After this initial watering let the pot become fairly dry before watering again, as the roots are only just forming and not yet absorbing very much. Once growth is obvious, then watering should be more frequent in early autumn, but slowing down as winter approaches, needing just monthly soaks until the leaves of spring demand increasing moisture in line with all the other bulbs.

At this point it is probably pertinent to mention feeding. If your compost is fresh then it is not necessary to feed in autumn, but as the leaves lengthen in spring a form of liquid fertilizer with a high potassium content, such as the commercial tomato types, can be used at half strength. This will encourage flower production for the next autumn. If the pot has only been top-dressed some growers advocate the application of a more evenly balanced fertilizer throughout the growing season, but again in a dilute strength.

You may be tempted to neglect the pots once they have flowered and concentrate your attention on those still in flower. This type of approach is not advised, as mould can soon take hold of the decaying flowers. These flowers rot very slowly in the high humidity and low temperatures of autumn, and the mould soon spreads to the leaves, which can result in the whole bulb being lost. Once the flower has finished, it may fall harmlessly onto the top dressing, but more often it becomes trapped in the structure of the leaves or within the coils of a cyclamen flower stem once it has been fertilized. A good pair of tweezers is essential to carefully remove these soft pieces of tissue without damaging the plant in any way.

Check too that all the bulbs have flowered and, if not, excavate the vacant space immediately. If the problem has been caused by a plant-eating larvae of some description, then the whole pot should be emptied and the roots washed clean of compost to remove any others that may be about to start their feeding. If the problem is rotting, then again remove the bulbs and discard any that are soft or show any sign of disease. Immerse the remaining bulbs in a liquid fungicide and then replant in fresh compost. Recent legislation has taken many pesticides and fungicides out of the gardener's armoury, so vigilance is going to be even more important in preventing disease and damage, with the gardener being more inclined to knock out the plant and inspect the compost. We will have to be quite uninhibited in our upending of pots to inspect the roots and become very handy with sharp scissors to remove suspicious material.

In early summer the bulbs will become dormant. Very few will require an absolutely dry summer rest; most will simply need a fairly dry compost, though do subject it to an artificial thunder shower with your watering can when the weather gets very hot and drying. Whatever the weather, the plunge material can be kept just moist, aided by shading inserted over the summer months. This shading can be made of plastic mesh, wooden slats or a white water-based paint – all best used externally. Internal shading is less effective in lowering the temperature, but is better than nothing.

During this dormant period the old withered leaves can be removed and seed collected. There are a few that ripen so quickly that they dehisce (split) before winter and so may catch the gardener out. The seeds of *Leucojum roseum* and many *Nerine* species are soon lost if not looked for in autumn and sown immediately. In fact autumn is the best season to sow all bulbous seed, coinciding as it does with the onset of rain and lower temperatures. Each genus and in some cases species has its unique method of dispersal, which the gardener soon gets to know and collects accordingly. Most autumn bulbs only mature their seed slowly and the ripeness coincides with the leaves dying away in the following summer. *Cyclamen hederifolium* takes up to ten months before the autumn-formed seed pods are ripe and the seed released for collection during the following July.

Frame cultivation

This is really free-range cultivation in plastic baskets with latticed sides (mainly used as pond baskets), so the roots are allowed out and in consequence often produce larger and stronger bulbs. There is a temptation to let these plants flower year after year, without lifting the basket to check their health or density. They do need less care, but must be checked regularly, or the basket may become so full it will burst or become a tourniquet that will damage the bulbs. Bulbs grown in this way can look very effective and provide great pleasure to growers who do not wish to have unsightly greenhouses in their gardens.

The construction of the frame must be strong, usually of brick, concrete blocks or old railway sleepers. If you use sleepers, the old preserving creosote may continue to leak out, particularly in hot weather, so line the inside with polythene to avoid any contamination. If your garden is plagued by moles, then lay 20mm (¾in) chicken wire under the whole structure, as their intrusion would be disastrous.

The site needs to be in as much light as possible and exposed to buoyant air movement, not one in a shady dank corner, where botrytis would spread very freely and the flowers all lean to search for light. The sides need not be more than 30cm (12in), but can be much higher to save stooping to admire and tend the plantings.

Once the sides are completed, a layer of hard core, such as broken bricks and concrete, can be tipped in and tamped down. The depth of this layer must leave 30cm (12in) of free board at the top. Ideally a covering of inverted turves should be fitted over the rubble, which will prevent your precious compost from being eroded too quickly into the gaps below. If you do not have turves then in-fill the rubble with a coarse gravel, which will aid drainage for years to come. The compost will need to reflect the ideal sort that you would use in a pot, but has to be mixed on a much larger scale. The well-tried mix of one part sieved soil, one part 4–5mm grit and one part of some organic component such as peat or mushroom compost, to which is added some organic fertilizer such as bone meal, will do well. Before planting, spread the compost to a few centimetres' (inches') depth over the whole area to cover the drainage material, which will then provide a bed for the lattice baskets.

Planting

With the frame prepared, the lattice pots can be planted and placed in position. Some thought needs to be given to the positioning of the pots, as height and leaf spread dictates how much room each container is allowed. It is a matter of choice whether autumn bulbs are mixed with their spring-flowering cousins. Do bear in mind the often tired nature of leaves that have withstood the storms of winter, which may detract from the later spring flowers. Also beware of planting rhizomes in a frame, as they soon invade the adjacent pots, giving you a very delicate extraction problem.

Once you have decided on the bulbs to use, lattice pots can be planted as a conventional pot. There will be some loss of compost, but as long as you pot up with slightly moist compost over a tray, this is not a problem. Labelling, as ever, is very important and an aluminium label bent around the top band of the lattice pot will preserve the name, planting date, etc. The 'graveyard' effect can be avoided by bending these labels downward and burying them until reference is needed. Another alternative, well suited to a geometric shape, is to draw a simple plan, which will not detract from the display.

Position the pots and in-fill around them, tamping the soil mix between each pot. If the sizes and depths vary, take care to arrange the rims to end up some 2cm (¾in) below the edge of the frame. Then cover the whole surface with 4–5mm grit of your choice and water well. In time there may be a little subsidence, which can be masked with more grit.

If you want an informal frame, which might be situated in the rest of the decorative garden, then plant without the use of pots and let the area develop more naturally, with self-sown seedlings and permanent plantings of dry-land plants like *Thymus membranaceus* and *Teucrium subspinosum*. If this area is small, the frame covering can be removed for much of the year, which will at least dilute the utilitarian aspect of the structure. The easy removal is also useful in times of drought, when the glass covering may dry the area too much for some bulbs.

Many bulb-frame bases are covered with an aluminium framework that is especially designed for the job, with sliding glass sides and roofs. These frames vary in height, but I would advise the reader always to buy the taller models, so that everything can be accommodated – even the torso of the gardener trying to answer the question 'Is it scented?' This type of frame is expensive, so gardeners have invented and constructed many different models of their own, using treated wood. These can be particularly useful where space is at a premium and non-standard shapes are needed.

The use of raised beds with glass covers was used in the 1930s by gardeners such as Gwendoline Anley. These were essentially raised beds for alpine plants, but even then she realized the potential for the successful cultivation of bulbous plants. Another adaptation has been the use of so-called 'Dutch Lights', a utilitarian wooden-framed glass light, which can be used as a sloping cover to the frame. Some inventive gardeners fit wheels so the lights can be lifted and rolled sideways for ease of access.

The growth and flowering of bulbous plants in this situation is prolific and so is the consequent seed production. This is obviously very beneficial for the gardener in ensuring the spread of a possibly rare and endangered plant. However the collection of seed is important for another reason: it prevents the pure stock being invaded by hybrid seedlings, which can be very hard to eliminate in the years to come. So even if you have more than enough for any friend or seed exchange, do collect the seed capsules before they dehisce.

A few seedlings will inevitably appear in neighbouring pots and need removing while still in flower. This may seem a drastic measure as the basket or pot has to be carefully emptied and the offending bulb removed. Tying a flag of wool to the stem as a marker for removal in the summer is fraught with difficulties, usually because the old stem snaps so readily and the exact bulb is hard to identify. For a similar reason, old top dressing and compost is best reused elsewhere as it always contains some seed. The resulting seedlings often surprise the gardener, by flourishing in unusual situations, like crevices and cracks, where a mature bulb would be too large to plant, or the gardener would not normally risk a planting. These chance seedlings often look very natural, far more so than the geometric positioning we often employ.

Each year the baskets need assessing as to their progress and as soon as there is a decline or overcrowding, then lift the basket in summer and repot the bulbs. Multiplication is often prodigious, only rarely are there any problems and these are usually due to the larval stage of some insect eating the bulb from the inside. If there is a decline, lift the basket immediately, as it is often possible to save some of the stock from destruction. As long as there is part of the basal plate left, then this may form new bulblets and roots in due course. Any damaged tissue must be carefully cut away and then dusted with a fungicide before replanting. This is only worth pursuing if the stock is precious and in short supply. If the basket is not to be lifted annually, then a dusting of a fertilizer such as bone meal in summer is advisable.

Raised beds

These are really bulb frames without any covering. Their fast drainage allows many bulbs to ripen in summer and not become waterlogged in winter, giving the bulb grower the chance to grow very many choice plants outside. The downside is the possible weather damage, not as great as often imagined, as the bulbs are grown harder and are often shorter and more robust. It is still possible to plant the bulbs in lattice pots, but many gardeners plant in groups and let the bulbs mingle with other plants. If you are plagued by rodents eating your bulbs, then a lattice pot covered with 10mm (½in) chicken wire defeats their incisors and has the advantage of being a hidden defence, not intrusive to the eye.

Plant the bulbs at a depth of approximately twice their diameter and bed them on a layer of sand – this is not as a protection, but as a guide to their whereabouts in future years when you come to dig nearby or begin to thin out the stock. Labelling is just as important as it is in the wider garden, if not more so.

Late summer is the time to check that the summer's luxuriant growth on neighbouring plants will not smother the autumn bulbs as they try to flower. If necessary, foliage can be pruned or held back to give the flowers space to emerge and flower freely. Some bulbs, particularly those that come from the southern hemisphere, react to a late summer storm and erupt from ground level to flower within just a few weeks. If the grower wishes to produce an artificial monsoon with a hose pipe for a garden opening, or for show purposes, bulbs can be induced to flower. Again, seedlings will abound; here they are welcome and provide a reserve for friends and garden visitors. The seed of most bulbous plants from the northern hemisphere will not ripen until the following summer, coinciding with the flowering of the spring bulbs. However, southern-hemisphere plants are generally much quicker with their production of seed, with some even ripening before the last flowers have faded.

The raised beds themselves are often more informal than the bulb frame, often curved and blending in with the features of the whole garden. Some are terraces on sloping ground, where only the down side is raised, presenting in a small area a choice of planting conditions, from fast to normal drainage. When the beds are constructed, drainage material must be incorporated in the compost, just as if a rock garden were being built. In the early years there will be some natural subsidence of the bed, which is not a problem with bulbs and can be turned into a positive help by topping up with fresh grit in which some granular or powdered fertilizer is incorporated.

After some years all fast-draining beds become consolidated and vital aeration is lost. It is then time to completely remake the bed with fresh compost. This is best undertaken in late summer for bulbous plants, but as these beds will usually have a mixed planting, a compromise to early autumn will ensure no stock is lost and root growth is quickly re-established. Some of the bulbs will be in flower or at least in bud, but if treated as simple bare-rooted plants and eased into place with a little coarse sand followed by a thorough watering, they do not suffer any long-term harm.

The open garden

In the 21st century there are more plants available to the gardener than ever before. New introductions are being made almost daily and commerce is inventing new names for old favourites. We can access them virtually, via the Internet, from CD-ROMs and Annual Plant Finders, and in reality from plant fairs, shows, garden centres and the ever-increasing number of small nurseries. Most gardeners, however, only have a finite amount of planting space and time in which to maintain this oasis of calm in a frantic world, so planning the garden and its planting must be made just as enjoyable as the garden itself.

Most gardens only have space for a few trees and shrubs and their selection is a very personal matter, but fraught with problems if the wrong choice is made, as any walk in a residential area will confirm. It is this garden framework, which provides the gradations of shade, shelter and dryness of soil in summer, that allows the bulb-grower to create diverse habitats. The great asset bulbs possess is their relatively slow colonization of ground and their periods of dormancy, which enable the gardener to clear any old foliage, thin the stock if required and feed the soil ready for the next season. There are exceptions to this description, however, with some onions and crocuses displaying a great tenacity, although this does depend on the soil structure and composition – so each gardener will have to work out his own *bête noire*.

The planting site is important, and is worth considering for some time before the trowel is wielded in earnest. In every garden there will be areas that provide very variable conditions which can be utilized by the gardener to good effect. Microclimates are, as the name suggests, very small areas which can be as clear-cut as the cool north side of a fence or wall, as opposed to the warm south side. There are other much less obvious features, however, that may go unnoticed and unused.

The angle of aspect of the land plays its part. In winter the first part of the garden to thaw after frost or the part that barely seems to freeze are worth investigating. Sometimes this may be down to good drainage or the lack of drainage, or overhead protection from an evergreen plant. It can be reflected or latent heat from a wall, especially one made of brick. Protection from the damaging effects of wind is important. Windy corners are problems and are best avoided. Once a framework of shrubs and trees is in place, it slows the wind more effectively than solid walls and fences that simply lift the air and then roll it back down the other side without any diminishing of power. There are some strong plastic meshes in quite discreet colours available to sieve the wind; they are not very beautiful, but worth considering in the short term.

The old adage of planting a bulb at twice its depth is usually very sound advice, but of course there are a few exceptions, which will be considered later. The chosen position should be forked to a greater depth to aerate the soil, and at the same time add a fertilizer such as bone meal and remove any root or weed that might contest the ground space. Then add a thin layer of sharp sand, into which the bulbs can be nestled. This does not unfortunately impede keeled slugs (*Tandonia budapestensis*), but does give the gardener warning of a cluster of bulbs while digging in later years and can prevent a tine impaling a bulb like a kebab.

Once the bulbs are planted, some form of labelling is essential, unless in a wild or woodland garden where the whole essence is informality. There have been numerous articles written about the merits of differing types of labelling material and how to avoid loss of clarity and labels being moved by some unseen force – the poor old blackbird is often blamed. Plastic labels are adequate in a pot but look very stark in the garden, and they soon become brittle and snap, or the surface breaks down and the markings are lost when exposed to the elements. Zinc and aluminium are still the best, being much more subtly coloured and lasting much longer, especially if they are attached to a length of galvanized wire, which can be pushed deep in the ground to avoid removal even by a gumbooted blackbird. Even the majority of the label can be buried, so lessening the visual impact. An HB pencil is still a very good marker, with some being quite legible even after 20 years. There are also small 12-volt hobby drills that can be fitted with diamond-tipped heads that are ideal for engraving metal labels. This can be quite a chore, but it may be worth considering for a particular open-ground genus or group of bulbs, like *Galanthus*, that are dormant for so much of the year.

Another minor irritant is the positioning of the label, whether behind or in front of the planting – make sure all who garden use the same regime! It seems logical to insert the label in front of the planted area, as most gardening seems to progress from the front to back of a border. Some gardeners who have large collections of bulbs utilize numbered tags attached to galvanized wire, recording the name and other details in a notebook or on a computer database. This is the least intrusive form of labelling, now the old lead-label marker of the last century has become a museum piece.

With ever more ingenious programs available for the computer some gardeners are cataloguing and mapping their gardens. Printed copies of plans produced in this way could be taken into the garden and therefore labels could become redundant. This approach does work well for collections of specific genera such as autumn *Crocus* or *Colchicum*, which tend to be cultivated ready for their flowering at the same time of year. Other gardeners may feel this is the kind of rigid discipline from which they are trying to escape.

PLANT ASSOCIATIONS

In the open garden the plant associations linked with bulbs are very important. It is easy to concentrate on the site and forget the flower colour next autumn. Many autumn bulbs flower without their leaves, which grow the following spring. This is not usually a problem, except in the case of bulbs that produce large leaves, like colchicums. In spring these leaves are bold and quite attractive, but by summer they need hiding as they decay. For these larger bulbs, plants like pulmonaria, grasses and ferns are good background foils for the autumn flowers and with the spring surge in growth are excellent at hiding the old bulb foliage.

The pulmonaria benefits from the removal of the often mildewed leaves in summer, soon growing new ones to compensate, so looking fresh by autumn. The polypodium fern and its numerous cultivars are still pristine in autumn because they only grow new fronds in summer, so any leaf-clearing from the bulb in summer is also the ideal time to remove the old leaves from the fern. The rhizomes are very compact and in some cases may need to be kept in check to avoid over-topping the bulbs. The rhizomes are easily removed and are very amenable to siting elsewhere. Grasses can provide the perfect background for the bulb flowers, with the seed heads looking at their best in autumn. The structure and contrast of grasses look good with the strong magenta pinks of the autumnal *Colchicums*.

Some of the autumn bulbs are very effective if planted and allowed to colonize quite large areas, either as monoculture or in partnership with another bulb flowering in a different season. *Cyclamen hederifolium* can look very effective when planted en masse, with a peak of flowering in September, and their attractive leaves can provide a dense ground cover from autumn until the following May. In summer the ground can be tidied, the seed capsules collected and a little general fertilizer incorporated with a mulch scattered over the site. The density of the leaves seems to preclude any companion planting and in any case there are only two months of bare ground before the first flowers begin to show in July. Siting is

Left: *Cyclamen hederifolium*

important, with colonies looking very much at home under deciduous trees, imitating their native haunts where they flower later in the autumn. They can also enliven areas under thin deciduous hedges or shrubs, where little else would thrive.

In spring many bulbs are used in drifts, but this is less often the case in autumn. Planning is easier in spring as there is often a bare canvas on which to create colour and form, with many more choices available. To achieve the same effect in autumn, the gardener has to be very firm about not slipping in odd plants in what appear to be bare areas during the year. Island beds are easily defined and when sited under a deciduous tree or shrub make ideal sites for planting certain bulbs. Surrounding grass can itself be an attractive backdrop to a planting. Some crocus species that set seed prolifically, such as *Crocus kotschyanus* and, to a lesser extent, *Crocus pulchellus* and *Crocus serotinus* subsp. *salzmannii,* can be planted and soon build up to give a freshness and colour to the October garden. Other crocuses, such as *Crocus nudiflorus, Crocus medius, Crocus goulimyi* and some forms of *Crocus cancellatus,* will increase vegetatively but will need the gardener's helping hand to cover large areas. *Crocus nudiflorus* is stoloniferous (horizontally spreading) when growing well and can even naturalize in grass as long as the sward is not cut too quickly in spring. The relatively small *Cyclamen coum,* which flowers in late winter, can happily mix with these plantings to extend the interest in the bed and again just leaves bare soil in high summer, when there is so much else to admire that the odd area of bareness does not look out of place.

Having suggested how the foliage of the large *Colchicums* could be hidden, there are instances where bold plantings can look quite stunning. *Colchicum tenorei,* with its tessellated (chequered) purplish-pink flowers, is an early-flowering species that has smaller leaves than many. This can be planted parallel to a low formal hedge such as *Buxus sempervirens* to provide a dramatic band of colour in early autumn, which is in turn muted by the dark green hedge. The largest species, generally selections of *Colchicum speciosum*, will do well in grassland in orchards or in the wild garden, where the leaves will never intrude and are soon lost in the long grass of springtime.

The few autumn-flowering snowdrops seem to thrive in quite sunny garden conditions. The flowers are usually fully open before the leaves begin to grow, and need careful placement. Small rock-garden plants are ideal companions for snowdrops, as is the autumn-flowering *Oxalis lobata* from South America. This bright yellow flower with clover-like leaves is very benign in spreading and recent winters have not damaged the plant in the least.

In early autumn many of the twining *Codonopsis* from Asia are at their best. These tuberous plants need a little extra attention to flower well, but will repay it handsomely with true blue through to pure white, campanula-like flowers, from August until October. The principle of planting the roots in shade and letting the stems rise into the sun, which applies to clematis, holds good

here. The white tubers can be planted in spring under deciduous shrubs like acers, where in summer the thin stems will twine their way to the light. Alternatively, plant them close to a wall or low fence, where the ground is often a little drier in winter than the surrounding area. They certainly do not like very wet winter conditions, so a little protection offered by other roots or shelter is essential. From the wall site they will climb freely into whatever host is above. By the first frosts of autumn the flowers will have finished and the stems can be cut back to ground level; in fact many species will have almost disappeared, simply leaving the stems to be removed. This almost ephemeral nature means there is no damage to the host. They are best acquired as dormant tubers as in growth they soon attach themselves to each adjacent plant and cannot easily be separated; a nightmare for nurseries. Seed is regularly set, but unfortunately is not usually ready to collect until quite late in the year, so it misses many of the amateur seed exchanges.

Alternatively, the tubers can be grown in humus-rich compost in pots or containers, either on their own or combined with other plantings. These plantings can be for spring,

using species such as woodland phlox or hepaticas, and codonopsis can be used to extend the season of interest. As the summer days lengthen the tiny stems will emerge and some framework will need to be inserted to host the climber. Hazel twigs or a spiral wire support are ideal, but you could arrange the container close to a wall or shrub and let the stems climb there. In winter the containers need to be quite dry, so are best placed under some protection; alternatively the tubers can be lifted, cleaned and stored in dry sand or vermiculite in a cool position until replanting in spring.

These plants are extremely delicate when just in growth, so when pricking out try a few together and do not try to extract each tiny tuber from its neighbour. Similarly, once you have a few tubers plant them in groups, so if an emerging stem is eaten, the loss is not noticable. Once the stems mature they become almost woody and molluscs seem to leave them alone. The tubers can flower in their second year from a single growing point, but in time the tuber will enlarge to become the size of a fist. Then it will have many growing points and will be far less vulnerable to attack.

PLANTING SITES

As mentioned earlier, every garden has some small areas that can be utilized by the gardener to extend the range of plants that can be grown in the open. Look beyond the obvious house and boundary walls or fences to any other ornamental or utilitarian constructions that present opportunities for planting. The quadrant between south and west is the most useful, as it will always be a little warmer and consequently suit some bulbs very well, particularly South African species, which have to grow during the short days of winter in low levels of light in the northern hemisphere.

These borders can be quite narrow and if situated near a house need to be checked for builders' rubbish and dug over deeply, as many of these bulbs are large with long, fleshy roots. For many years gardeners have grown *Nerine bowdenii* and *Amaryllis belladonna* in these situations; it is time to be a little more adventurous and experiment with some of the newer bulbs that are becoming available. As most gardeners are cautious people and hate to lose a plant, grow the stock from seed and then plant out some of the resulting bulbs, keeping a reserve in the greenhouse or frame. If the experiment is successful then the contents of the pot in the greenhouse can also be planted out straight from the pot with consequent gain of space in the usually overcrowded greenhouse. Planting out lessens the stresses imposed on the bulbs, as there will be a very short exposure to drying as the planting can be done at the optimum time.

Failure can occur when stock that is grown in nearly neat peat is planted in the garden. The bulb will have grown very well in this medium in the controlled conditions of a nursery, but when planted in the ordinary garden soil there is a problem of incompatibility. Roots can struggle to gain a hold in the firmer surrounding soil and may corkscrew around the planting hole, but worse still, the peat tends to dry out and shrink more quickly than the soil, leaving a gap between the two mediums with obvious results. The best remedy is to wash the peat-based compost completely off the bulb and plant as a dry bulb. If the bulb is in root, still wash, but pot into your own soil-based mix and grow on in a shady place for a few weeks before planting out.

The building may have overhanging eaves, which give a surprising amount of frost protection. If the wall has no overhang, then mobile glass or glass substitute covers can be put in place when a hard frost is forecast. Their designs are legion and many reflect the ingenuity of the grower, but the principle of retaining the heat and stopping it radiating into the night air are the same. If this bed is close to the house the aesthetic aspect is important, so, instead of a man-made cover, an airy cover of straw or coarse bark can give some insulation to the bulbs and it can be removed as soon as the worst of the frost has passed. Horticultural fleece, often used to wrap shrubs to protect them from frost and wind damage, can easily be pegged down over the bed to give the same type of effect. A similar benefit can be achieved by the judicious planting and pruning of an evergreen shrub directly to the north of the bed. Conifers can work for a few years, but the density of their roots can become a problem in the longer term.

If paths and access to the house preclude these beds, a purpose-built bed with protection can be built. This is essentially an attractive frame that does not look too utilitarian in the main garden. Building materials need to be in sympathy with the house and surroundings, but brick is nearly always acceptable, especially as there is always a choice of colour. The idea is to protect the planting area during the winter months and then remove the lights for the bulk of the year, leaving the site looking like the traditional raised bed. When planning this bed, always design the largest possible as so many plants, not just bulbs, will thrive here that space will soon be at a premium.

A design that has worked without any maintenance for many years is a brick raised bed, where the depth is just under the length of a Dutch light. The rear of the brick bed is built up to provide the growing height needed. The width is determined by the number of lights you wish to accommodate. The back wall can be ventilated by leaving gaps between some bricks. In the top row of bricks, incorporate some spigots to hold the lights during periods of strong wind. The front of the lights need wooden legs bolted or screwed in place to lift the lights off the bed, allowing for shorter plants, good air movement and free run-off of rain. As long as the lights are fixed to the back wall the front legs do not seem to need fixing. This structure could also be adapted to suit any modern transparent sheeting. Always face the open side to the quadrant between the south-east and the south-west to obtain as much light and heat as possible. The bed will not require watering during the winter as

transpiration is so low at this time of the year. As a result many presumed tender plants are quite hardy down to -10°C (14°F), whereas those in saturated soil soon rupture and die.

Moving away from man-made constructions, some bulbs are able to be naturalized in grassland. This land has to be cut or grazed at the appropriate season to enable the plant to complete its annual life-cycle. As mentioned earlier, colchicums will generally thrive in these conditions. The treatment of larger areas can be quite drastic, even to the extent of letting the late-summer grass cut distribute the seed. Some bulbs will be damaged but many survive to extend the colony. The other genus to provide autumn colour in grass is *Crocus*. The afore-mentioned *Crocus nudiflorus* and others such as *Crocus speciosus* and *Crocus ochroleucus* can be naturalized in grass. Here the grass has to be cut a little shorter in late summer, to give the flowers a chance to show well from a distance.

This form of gardening is not a lazy option, as mowing and grass removal has to coincide with the dormant period and the last cut of summer timed just before the flowers emerge. Planting in these areas, often at the edges of the garden where they blend well with native hedges or in areas of old fruit trees, looks less artificial than many gardening endeavours. The native plants in the grassland can be ignored, as the more unpleasant ones like the stinging nettle soon succumb to regular mowing.

The planting of the bulbs is best done at random, not in geometric designs. Throwing the bulbs into the area and then planting where they fall is often suggested, but can be very time-consuming, so as a compromise, lift off a slice of turf with a spade and then plant by trowel. The spadework can be at random and in any case some bulbs will thrive while others dwindle to give a natural look very quickly. There are various bulb planters available, from small hand cylinders to larger models that are pushed in by the foot; all are linked to a frame at waist level. The hand tool soon leads to an aching wrist, so is not suitable for large plantings. Effective, but less random, is a slit trench levered out by a spade, used to good effect for larger bulbs, but less so for smaller, as they tend to roll over in the bottom of a diminishing slit in the soil.

By planting other bulbs, these naturalized areas can also become highlights in winter and spring, as long as there is a dormant period in summer to enable the grass to be cut on a few occasions, gradually lowering the cut to prepare a background for the flowers of autumn. The cycle can be maintained by planting *Galanthus* sp. and *Eranthis hyemalis* for winter, with a larger choice of plants such as *Fritillaria meleagris*, *Narcissus bulbocodium*, *Ophrys apifera* or *Ornithogalum nutans* for spring. In general the bulbs of meadowland, including short snowmelt swards, can be utilized to picturesque effect in these semi-natural surroundings. If stocks allow, then plants such as *Spiranthes cernua* and *Spiranthes spiralis*, the diminutive white orchids of autumn, could be added, as these autumn Ladies' Tresses are quite prolific in their production of tubers when grown in pots.

AN A-Z OF AUTUMN BULBS

This section gives a comprehensive view of the autumn-flowering bulbous plants available. Many are obtainable through commercial sources, but some will have to be hunted down from specialist growers and then may only be available as seed. This is not really bad news as seed-grown stock should not suffer any stress in transplanting and also gives you the chance to experiment with growing conditions. The aim for most people is to find the right conditions to grow the plants in the open garden, or at least within man-made features in the garden.

Aconitum

Just one aconitum fits the criteria, being tuberous and autumn-flowering, but one of great beauty and substance, if only it were in cultivation.

Aconitum hookeri
Most of this genus are quite rightly treated as tuberous border perennials; however this alpine species, found from south-western China through to Nepal, has small tubers which can fit in a bulbous growing regime. Some 10cm (4in) tall, this has quite large purple-blue flowers, produced in early autumn. The tubers are best potted and then exposed to a long cold winter and a damp growing season. Rarely available and even then only from seed, but worth every effort to maintain in cultivation.

Left: *Allium thunbergii* (white form) (see over page)

Allium

A huge genus, nearly all from the northern hemisphere. From the gardener's point of view they range from the most beautiful to the most pestilential of all garden bulbs. The autumn-flowering species do not present problems with excessive seed and bulbil production; all are quite demure and controllable, with the exception of *Allium tuberosum*. The other three small autumnal onions will never become weeds in cool, temperate gardens and have proved easy and attractive additions to the autumn garden or greenhouse.

Below: *Allium callimischon*

Allium callimischon subsp. haemostictum

A small Cretan onion, this species has loose umbels of white or pale pink flowers with distinct dark red spots, which repays closer inspection as it is really a very attractive plant. In Crete, *Allium callimsichon* subsp. *haemostictum* flowers without its leaves, but, in common with *Allium callimischon* subsp. *callimischon* and a number of other autumnal bulbs, produces short leaves with the flowers in more northern gardens. The subspecies *callimischon*, found on the Greek mainland, is without the red spots and is also a little taller. Both subspecies make excellent pot plants but are equally at home in a sunny raised bed. The flower stems are formed in early summer and are straw-coloured, so be careful not to deadhead this seemingly inert stem before it flowers in October.

Allium thunbergii

A semi-evergreen whose leaves have a remarkably similar appearance to culinary chives. The bulb is slim with virtually perennial roots and a flower stem to 15cm (6in). The loose umbel of rose-purple flowers appears in October and November and has exerted stamens which give an almost powder-puff-like look to the heads.

There is an American selection, *Allium thunbergii* 'Ozawa', which has been given an Award of Merit, but this seems to be very little different from the species in cultivation. The white form is particularly attractive. This Japanese and Korean onion comes from low mountainous areas and can be easily cultivated in a pot or the open garden in humus-rich conditions.

Allium tuberosum

An easy plant to grow, which thrives in sun or shade. The white flowers are packed in a hemispherical umbel on a 30–40cm (12–16in) stem, flowering over a long period from August until October. It is found widely in south-eastern Asia, where it is often used in salads. Unlike all the other autumnal onions, it is best to dead-head this one to avoid too many self-sown seedlings.

Allium virgunculae

Another Japanese onion, with slender grass-like foliage that flowers in October and November. The plant is 15cm (6in) tall with pink, quite substantial flowers in a loose umbel. It is easily grown in a pot or in a sunny position in the open garden. It is almost evergreen so best split up when just dormant in winter or early spring. This plant was awarded an AM in 1983.

Amaryllis

Here is a genus of just one from the coastal hills and stream banks of the south-western corner of the Cape Province, South Africa.

Amaryllis belladonna

A large bulb with a large flower to match, which grows rapidly once autumn rains begin. This South African bulb is proving to be quite hardy, but does need to be planted next to a south-facing wall or fence to produce flowers regularly. The bulb needs to be planted with the neck just visible, from which in August the buds begin to emerge

Above: *Amaryllis belladonna*

and grow quickly to 60–80cm (24–32in) before up to five trumpet-shaped flowers open. The usual selection is pale pink, but selections are available with darker flowers and stems. *Amaryllis belladonna* 'Hathor' is a particularly attractive white form, with lime green buds. The strap-shaped leaves begin to grow in November and can need protection if hard frost is forecast. Fleece is useful here and more easily removed than straw. Even if some leaves are frost-damaged the plant seems to continue to send up sufficient leaf area to prepare next year's flower stems.

Viable seed is often set and needs immediate sowing to grow, producing leaves the same winter. Flowering, however, is less quick, with six to seven years needed before the first bud is formed. A rich growing medium helps to speed up the process and variation in coloration is always possible in these progeny. At this nursery stage, frame or greenhouse protection is required.

Amaryllis × Amarcrinum
Amaryllis × Amarine
Amaryllis × Amarygia

These three hybrids, between *Crinum*, *Nerine* and *Brunsvigia* respectively, are autumn-flowering and occasionally offered for sale. Each is a very large bulb that requires a sheltered sunny aspect to succeed. Some are distinct, but × *Amarine* seems to be little more than a tall-growing form of *Nerine bowdenii*, with little influence of *Amaryllis* in the cross.

Anemone

There seems to be only one anemone that flowers in autumn: some strains of *Anenome coronaria* regularly flower in October and November. These are very striking and the equal of the more usual spring production.

Anemone coronaria
The flowering period of this so-called poppy anemone from the Mediterranean basin spans six months. There are selections that

Above: *Anemone coronaria*
Below: *Anemone coronaria* in the Peloponnese, Greece

flower in October and November as long as they are given well-drained sunny sites to induce flowering. Alternatively, pot cultivation suits this knobbly tuber, which is not too dry and desiccating. The flowers can be as varied as their spring cousins – red, purple, pink and every shade in between and even a few semi-doubles, all with the marvellous contrasting black anthers. The leaves look a little like flat-leaved parsley and are present at flowering.

Arum

The arums are a group of plants that are grown for a combination of reasons. It may be the unusual, architecturally attractive spathe (bract) and spadix (flower), or the beautifully veined and marked leaves, or finally the stunning display of the cylindrical spike of orange to red berries. These features appear for periods spanning many months, some of which coincide with autumn. The descriptions below will describe the whole plant for completeness, but concentrate on the autumn features. If they are planted in sites that suit their needs, all these species are extremely easy to grow.

Arum concinnatum
From the southern Aegean islands including Crete and south-western Turkey. This species is often referred to as needing protection from frost but a particularly attractively marked leaf form from Crete has thrived in a raised, part-shaded bed in the UK for over ten years. The leaves are dark green and slightly glossy, with blotches of silver grey and usually unfurl in October, and like many arums this very attractive foliage lasts for many months. The sagittate leaves can reach 50cm (20in) in length and half as wide.

Arum cyrenaicum
The leaves sprout in early autumn, just 20cm (8in) long and a mid-green colour with indented veins and a purple-stained stem. It thrives in an unrestricted bulb frame, which is open to the elements in winter. This plant, hailing from Libya, grows in shaded niches under boulders, with *Cyclamen rohlfsianum*. As with so many plants, the original home conditions can successfully be adapted in cool temperate climates. However, trying to grow *Cyclamen rohlfsianum* in similar conditions would be one step too far.

Arum dioscoridis
A long-cultivated plant with a handsome purple blotched spathe in spring. The typical arrow-shaped leaves are a mid-green and produced in early autumn. Totally hardy, this plant has a very noticeable malodorous smell when in flower.

Arum hygrophilum
The slim, shiny green leaves spear through the soil in mid-autumn, up to 40cm (16in) in length and only about one-quarter the width. It grows around the eastern Mediterranean. It is always assumed to be tender, but seems simply to need a damp situation with a little tree canopy for rudimentary protection. The unscented inflorescence can emerge late in autumn, if the season has been particularly mild and damp.

Arum italicum subsp. *italicum* 'Marmoratum'

This species can give a show in autumn on two counts. In early autumn the very attractive berries on 30cm (12in) stems are eye-catching and last well until very ripe, when they are eaten by birds. This is no bad thing, as too many seedlings in one place detract from the display. The most commonly found selection is often called *Arum italicum* 'Pictum'; unfortunately this has never been formally published and should be identified as *Arum italicum* subsp. *italicum* 'Marmoratum'. This is a worthwhile distinction as the true *Arum pictum* is so very distinct. *Arum italicum* subsp. *italicum* 'Marmoratum' has very well-marked leaves with veins of silvery grey, cream or yellow, depending on the selection, all appearing by the end of autumn. The cultivar 'Chameleon' has most unusually marked leaves with silvery swirls and a mixed green background.

Arum maculatum

This species, also known as Lords and Ladies in the United Kingdom, seems to be present in many gardens without gardeners' intervention. Birds enjoy the berries and soon spread the seeds at random. It is attractive but rather too invasive in controlled areas of the garden, and is best left in hedge bottoms and wilder places. There are forms with black spots on the plain green leaves, which themselves vary considerably in size and shape – not surprising as the plant is found throughout Europe.

Right: *Arum italicum*

Above: *Arum pictum*

Arum orientale

From Eastern Europe, this autumn-leafing variety has quite broad, plain green leaves up to 25cm (10in) long. A damp-growing species, very at home planted with trees and shrubs and even alongside water.

Arum pictum

This is the outstanding arum for autumnal display, as, unusually, the inflorescence and leaves occur in this season. In early autumn the purple spathe and even darker purple spadix emerge surrounded by thick glossy dark-green leaves which are distinctly marked in the best selections. In these the veins stand out as creamy-white or a silvery-grey network which seems to intensify as the season develops. *Arum pictum* 'Primrose Warburg' is one such selection and well worth seeking out. As the species is from Tuscany and the islands of the central Mediterranean, it is best to plant in a sheltered site with good drainage; however, so far, a temperature of -10°C (14°F) has failed to damage the leaves.

Biarum

A small genus of about 15 species of autumn-flowering tubers that look rather like small arums, except that they flower nakedly. The leaves follow quickly and are far less impressive than those of their larger relatives, without any of the arrow-like lobes at the base. They suit pot cultivation as they fit the typical Mediterranean regime and are not too large. They can also be grown in bulb frames and well-drained, sunny beds. They are quite hardy. The spathes have little or no stems, so sit at ground level and, like other Araceae, emit a fetid smell.

Biarum carduchorum
This mainly Turkish species has a deep purple-black spathe of which the lower quarter forms a tube. The spadix is up to 20cm (8in) long and is just contained within the spathe.

Biarum davisii
The most unusual of all these peculiar plants because it is sweet-smelling. It has a squat, bottle-shaped spathe, creamy yellow with purple-pink spots on the inside, flowering in mid-autumn. The curved spadix is a dull reddish-brown and only just protrudes from the mouth of the spathe. Short leaves emerge much later in winter. The species is found in Crete and southern Turkey, with the Turkish plant larger and more easily flowering. Their size ideally suits them to pot culture.

Biarum eximium
In this Turkish species the deep purple spathe leans back from the tall black spadix. The 10cm (4in) spathe, which is quite velvety, forms a cup at the base, and the whole effect is quite eye-catching. The leaves follow reaching 20cm (8in), part of which is a stem.

Biarum spruneri
This Greek species flowers very early in autumn and then retires below ground for a few months before the leaves appear in winter. The dark reddish-purple spathe about 20cm (8in) tall is very erect with a darker spadix of similar length. This plant begins to flower before the bulb grower has thought of watering, but is very easy to cultivate and tolerant of neglect.

Below: *Biarum tenuifolium*

Above: *Codonopsis vinciflora*

Biarum tenuifolium

This has a widespread distribution around the Mediterranean and varies in appearance accordingly. All are easy to cultivate, spreading by freely produced offsets. The spathe is usually purple, but a variety *abbreviatum* is green; all are about 20cm (8in) long with an even longer spadix. They are scattered over terra-rossa soils, usually at quite low altitude. They grow freely in temperate gardens, but do require a sunny spot to flower freely in early autumn, where the leaves can follow soon after flowering. If grown in a pot they will need annual repotting to accommodate the tubers' increase.

Codonopsis

Many of the climbing members of this large family of Asian plants flower well into autumn. They are tuberous and best sited at the base of a wall or under a deciduous shrub where excess water is rare. They can be pot-grown and sited under a shrub for the growing season or given twigs or metal coils for support. They like a moisture-retentive soil and, rather like clematis, thrive where the roots are cool and the flowers are in the sun. In winter the old foliage is easily removed and the containers can be stored in a cool

place, even stacked on one another under the greenhouse benching to conserve space. Then in spring the tubers can be teased out and replanted for the season ahead. Alternatively, the tubers can be knocked out in late autumn and stored in dry sand or vermiculite in a cool place until the spring planting. It is as well to check the tubers occasionally for any sign of rot.

These plants are rarely offered commercially as their twining nature means disentanglement of mature plants is virtually impossible without considerable damage. However if treated as 'bulbs' and planted while dormant, this climbing feature is a virtue because there is no need to train by tying or staking.

Codonopsis forrestii

This species, from the mountains of south-western China, is found in light woodland and can climb to 3m (10ft) in cultivation, but is easily trained over any aerial construction, natural or man-made. The large, true blue, five-petalled, star-shaped flowers are very freely produced, reaching their peak in early September. The bud is reminiscent of a *Platycodon grandiflorum* (balloon flower); however, the pale blue of the bud belies the strong blue of the flower, which, when revealed, spreads to some 6cm (2½in) in diameter. The thin twining stems bear quite thick, almost succulent, slightly toothed lanceolate leaves, with the flowers produced singly on short lateral stems. Seed is usually set in large capsules and is best collected and

Left: *Codonopsis forrestii*

stored for sowing in early spring, when the delicate germinations will grow on without check. The fine nature of the young stems of the seedlings are best left to grow on undisturbed for a season, before separating the young tubers and potting on in winter, when the entangled foliage is absent.

Codonopsis meleagris

The only late-flowered, non-climbing codonopsis that continues to flower into autumn. Seedlings that occur around the parent may be hybrids with other non-climbing codonopsis that flowered a little earlier. So do care for the parent: it can develop a large carrot-like tuber and have many lax shoots that branch, each producing a hanging straight-sided bell-shaped flower. These flowers are chequered purple on a yellowy-green background, with a stunning purple interior. They can be propagated by taking a small piece of tuber with a growing shoot in spring and growing on as a cutting. This at least ensures a pure stock.

Codonopsis vinciflora

From a similar area to *Codonopsis forrestii*, but from greater altitude, where it is found growing among low shrubs. The white tubers can in time become quite large and knobbly, producing many growth points – a useful trait as the new soft tissue is vulnerable to molluscs in the first few weeks of growth, after which it hardens and becomes quite strong. This plant seems to be one of the toughest for general outdoor cultivation, thriving in large containers that remain outside without any protection in winter.

This species is a twining plant to 2m (6ft), with starry blue flowers, some 4cm (1½in) in diameter, which are freely produced in late summer and early autumn. Occasionally a white form has been offered, but this always seems to be the summer-flowering *Codonopsis grey-wilsonii* 'Himal Snow'. *Codonopsis vinciflora* is clearly identified by the short sepals that never enclose the bud, whereas other climbers have much larger tightly fitting sepals at the bud stage. The leaves are smaller, thinner and less pointed than *Codonopsis forrestii*.

Colchicum

This is one of the major genera for autumn display. The large-flowered forms of pink to purple, and occasionally white, flowers are reliably produced every year, enlivening the flagging late summer and autumn border. Admittedly they do produce large leaves in spring, which by summer are turning yellow and need removing, but any gardener worth his salt should be able to plan neighbouring plantings to hide this natural process. These leaves are quite a feature; they look almost like a plain hosta leaf for a month and then high summer foliage, with its plethora of foliage and flowers, can hide their decay.

To flower well, they do need direct sun for at least part of the day. In shade they become etiolated and fall over quickly. The corms can be easily moved without any check just before or even at flowering, as the roots are only just beginning to grow at this time. To counsel perfection, they are best lifted as the foliage dies down, sorted and replanted in enriched soil with the top of their necks just visible. They travel well as dry corms, even flowering in a dry state while waiting to be purchased. They can still be rescued to grow on quite well, with the leaves not appearing until spring. The naming of some cultivars has become a little muddled, with one selection having at least three names. Small bulb nurseries stock the widest and most interesting selections. It is true that names are easier to collect than the true selection, so perseverance will be needed. It is even worthwhile taking a few flowers picked from your own garden for comparison, but do let the nursery gardener know first, or it may become embarrassing explaining why you have a handful of flowers!

The positioning of plants is a very personal matter, but considerations of colour matching and contrasting with the quite unusual rose-purple of many colchicums is important. Green is always a good foil for these plants, perhaps using the many selections of *Polypodium* ferns available. Shorter selections such as *Polypodium interjectum* 'Cornubiense' can be very useful in supporting colchicum flowers and look fresh and attractive in their own right. Strangely, yellow can make an excellent background, with grasses and sedges such as *Carex elata* 'Aurea' (Bowles' 'Golden Sedge') and *Milium effusum* 'Aureum' (Bowles' 'Golden Grass'), highlighting the early autumn garden. The grass does seed around quite profusely, but is easily removed if it is in the wrong place, whereas the sedge has to be planted and is best extended by careful division in spring.

Another useful associate is pulmonaria. It can be rather too invasive, but this can be remedied by judicious use of the spade in spring and a complete removal of the spring foliage in summer, which incidentally removes botrytis and prepares them very well for the fresh autumn flourish of perfect leaves. The silvery selections are excellent as a background to the deep purple forms such as *Colchicum speciosum* 'Atrorubens'. Thinking of silver foliage, some of the artemisias look perfect as accompaniments; plants like *Artemisia absinthium* 'Lambrook Silver' and *Artemisia nutans* are fully clothed with leaves in late summer and by spring will need some pruning to encourage new growth, so allowing the colchicum leaves a free run.

Colchicum speciosum and *Colchicum autumnale* naturally occur in meadows, so planting them in semi-rough grass is an option. They can look very attractive as long as the grass is cut in August prior to their flowering and left until late the following June to give the leaves their full growth cycle. Planting drifts in between large shrubs, even under a thin canopy of mature trees, can be quite stunning and here no particular plant association is needed and the leaves will never become a problem. They will need lifting and replanting every three or more years. The annually replaced corms always form in the same place as their parents, which have withered away, and with offset corms forming next to the flowering corms the whole site becomes very crowded and flowering suffers. When replanting it is a good time to remove the keeled slugs, the bane of underground storage organs – they may be inside the old brown tunic and do considerable damage to the actual corm. The brown tunics are a downward extension of the leaves and over a number of years build up and inhibit flowering. These tunics seem to be impervious to rotting and become almost bark-like if left for many years.

This is a genus of over 60 species, with the large-flowered and large-leaved species generally from meadows and woodland banks, whereas the small-flowered species are mostly found in drier and rockier situations. After mentioning some of the problems with cultivar identification, the species too, are a challenge. The anthers are often cited as aids to naming, but some change colour with age. The leaves, also diagnostic, are often absent at flowering time, so another useful guide is not available unless a return is made to the exact location in spring. The corm shape and size is also diagnostic. A trawl through old literature highlights dozens of discarded names and still new ones are being found and registered with great regularity. In short, the genus needs sorting, but with such problems it will be a painstaking and lengthy task.

In his *A Handbook of Crocus and Colchicum,* E A Bowles wrote of these problems for the gardener in 1924 and then again in the revised edition in 1952. Since then many short articles have been written and sections within books devoted to the genus. In 1996 and 1997 the RHS undertook trials to assess colchicums for the AGM. This was a very useful step to correct naming and picking the best for garden-worthiness.

The descriptions of the plants will first cover the middle-sized species and selections and then the large-flowered species and selections that are for the open garden and finally the smaller species. Mention will be made of awards throughout.

Middle-sized species and selections

Colchicum agrippinum

This old hybrid, probably between *Colchicum variegatum* and *Colchicum autumnale*, is one of the easiest colchicums to grow. It is moderately tall and does flop, but produces so many flowers from one corm, it can be forgiven. The flowers are distinctly tessellated pink and white with purple-tipped anthers held on quite long white perianth tubes. It is far taller than *C. variegatum* and much easier to grow. The leaves have slightly undulate margins, and are quite compact, with a tendency to rise from the horizontal.

Right: *Colchicum agrippinum*

Above: *Colchicum autumnale*

Colchicum atropurpureum

A relatively small-flowered plant, which opens pink and then darkens to a deep reddish-purple. In fact the buds emerge white, causing some consternation before the quick colour change. As it is quite small, a raised bed or even a pot is suitable for cultivation. The name 'atropurpureum' does seem to be at odds with the pale colour of some of the seedlings. These seedlings seem indistinguishable from *Colchicum autumnale*.

Colchicum autumnale

The only colchicum species native to the UK, this species is found mostly in areas of rich meadowland, with notable sites under the stewardship of County Wildlife Trusts. Also found throughout Europe, *Colchicum autumnale* has flowers to 5cm (2in) long, with quite thin, pale pink starry segments. Luckily for the gardener, many selections have been made of more substantial and eye-catching forms. There are some attractive neat doubles, both mid-pink (*Colchicum autumnale* 'Pleniflorum') and white (*Colchicum autumnale* 'Alboplenum') Any white selections, of which many occur naturally in colonies in the UK, are really a creamy-white, which produce successive flowers from a single corm, with a ring of intact flowers lying around the later upright ones.

Colchicum autumnale 'Elizabeth'

This is an early-flowering form from the Alpes Maritimes. It is very distinct with pale pink segments and was collected by Dick Trotter in the company of E A Bowles in the first half of the 20th century. It is named after Elizabeth Parker-Jervis, his daughter, famous herself for a nursery and garden which specialized in colchicums at the end of the 20th century.

Colchicum autumnale 'Nancy Lindsay' (pannonicum 'Nancy Lindsay') AGM ♈

An excellent selection of good vigour, for which the naming has now finally been settled. It is a fine, strong, plain pink, with a white line beginning at the base of each segment. The tube is dark pink and the leaves, which appear in spring, are relatively small. This selection is believed to come from Eastern Europe and is very reliable and tolerant of many garden situations.

Colchicum byzantinum AGM ♈

An ancient plant of unknown origin, which has some affinity with *Colchicum cilicicum*, with a central pale stripe from the base of each segment which tapers towards the tip. The unscented flowers are also narrower but taller, with a long perianth tube. Each segment has a tiny tip of purple, a feature that has been passed on to the white selection *Colchicum byzantinum* 'Innocence'. The leaves are some of the largest seen on colchicums, with deep veins that are quite attractive in spring. A very reliable plant, which tolerates a wide range of conditions.

Colchicum kotschyi

This Middle Eastern species is very early-flowering for an autumn bulb – it is often in flower by late August. It is slow to increase and may be better suited to bulb-frame cultivation, but does hold its own in a sunny border. The flower segments, which are up to 5cm (2in) long, open widely in sun and are usually pinkish-purple, but white forms are quite common. It has yellow anthers. The leaves are relatively small, reaching 15cm (6in) in an ascending fashion.

Colchicum laetum hort. 'Pink Star' AGM ♈

This is not the true species, which is much smaller, so by way of differentiation the epithet 'Pink Star' includes all the highly floriferous plants that used to be simply called *Colchicum laetum*. This plant is probably a selection of *Colchicum byzantinum*; it certainly has the pale stripe, but not the purple tips to each segment. The segments are pale purple-pink with quite rounded ends and are often horizontally displayed in great profusion.

Above: *Colchicum laetum* hort 'Pink Star'

Colchicum 'Little Woods'. (*C. 'Intermediate Woods'*)

One of the later-flowering selections into October, which has segments wider than *Colchicum autumnale*, but is of a similar size. The perianth tube is pure white with light pink petals with lines. The stigmata has a dark purple tip. An attractive compact plant that stands well, being quite weather-resistant.

Colchicum tenorei (*C. lusitanicum*) AGM ♔

To the gardener there seems little if any difference between these two colchicums, with *Colchicum tenorei* finding most favour. It is one of the first to flower, often showing

well in late August. It is a compact plant with lightly tessellated flowers, with an obvious red stigmata, and is found in Italy and the Iberian peninsula.

Large-flowered species and selections

The following section is devoted to the large species and hybrids that are best grown in the open garden, in groups or drifts. One bonus of growing colchicums is the discipline needed in preparing an area to look at its best, for their display. By late summer much luxuriant foliage often needs attention and the buds of colchicums dictate that this work cannot be left. The overhanging foliage needs trimming, weeds need removing, and then the ground can be aerated and given a general fertilizer such as bone meal. This sets the display off very well and usually leads to other nearby work, which keeps the garden generally in trim.

Colchicum bivonae (*C. bowlesianum*, *C. sibthorpii*, *C. latifolium*)

A variable, large-flowered species found from Italy eastwards to Turkey. Typically found as a bright purple-pink, highly tessellated flower which is quite slow to increase in northern climes. Unfortunately the rules of nomenclature rule out the recognition of E A Bowles, who did so much to improve our knowledge of this genus, firstly by cultivation, then by his writings.

Left: *Colchicum tenorei*
Right: *Colchicum bivonae*

Colchicum cilicium

A most satisfactory plant, with deep rose-lilac flowers and barely any chequering. It has short perianth tubes, giving the flower the strength to withstand the weather. It has a very noticeable white line down the centre of each segment, which tapers to the tip, forming a slim star. The long white styles have an obvious purple tip. Soon after flowering the large leaves begin to grow and are quite well developed by winter. *Colchicum cilicicum* 'Purpureum' has very pronounced purple tips to each segment, which contrast starkly with the pure white perianth tubes. This Turkish plant is one of the very best and because it is a species it comes true from seed.

Colchicum davisii (PD 26938)

A relatively newly named, large-flowered colchicum species, originating from Turkey. The corms are elongated with a number of growing points and they seem to pull themselves down as the years pass, so extra care is needed when lifting is undertaken. The flowers are very pale pink and conspicuously tessellated with a large white throat. The anthers are prominent and a bright yellow colour. The leaves do not appear until spring.

Colchicum giganteum (C. speciosum var. illyricum)

The experts are unsure about whether this is a distinct species; more fieldwork is required in Turkey. There is a distinct selection in cultivation that flowers very early in August. The buds are white as they emerge, but soon open to reveal quite pale pinkish-purple funnel-shaped flowers with a slight twist in each segment, on a white tube. Still cultivated is *Colchicum giganteum* ACW 2337, a strong-growing, early flowering plant which for garden purposes seems quite unique.

Opposite: *Colchicum cilicium*
Right: *Colchicum cilicium* 'Purpureum'

Above: *Colchicum macrophyllum*
Opposite: *Colchicum giganteum*

Colchicum macrophyllum

A very large, funnel-shaped flower, highly tessellated with white contrasting with the rosy-purple in the pattern. The throat is paler, often white. This plant hails from around the Aegean Sea and may be a little tender, or may need a warm rest period to flower well. Like many plants, their original altitude and site influences their chances of success when grown further north. Some selections flower every year without any protection as long as the site is sunny, and there is some shelter from the north. They are best outside as the vernal leaves are huge, up to 40cm (16in) long and nearly half as wide. They are pleated and actually very attractive in youth.

Colchicum speciosum

This meadowland plant from Turkey, Iran and the Caucasus is the pick of all the autumnal colchicums. The flowers are freely produced, substantial goblets up to 20cm (8in) tall, with a range of colours from quite pale pinkish-purple to a deep shiny purple, many with very noticeable white throats. All the flowers have yellow anthers.

Apart from the selections of the species and a few varieties there are many hybrids that have *Colchicum speciosum* as one parent.

All are followed by glossy leaves in spring, which reach up to 25cm (10in) long by 10cm (4in) wide.

Colchicum speciosum var. *bornmuelleri*

This name is regularly misapplied to early-flowering forms of *Colchicum speciosum*, but should really only apply to the plants with purple or purple-brown anthers, which usually have white throats. The green perianth tube is not diagnostic and can be found in populations of *Colchicum speciosum*.

The leaves of *Colchicum speciosum* var. *bornmuelleri* are approximately half as wide as they are long, providing another useful aid to their identification.

Colchicum speciosum 'Album' AGM ♔

This selection is the finest of all colchicums. The flower is a long-lasting, pure white, perfectly proportioned goblet, supported by a lime-green perianth tube, making it one of the finest of all the autumnal flowers. This selection is over a hundred years old and came from the renowned nursery of Backhouse of York, which closed in 1955.

Colchicum speciosum 'Atrorubens'

This dark selection with a white throat makes a fine contrast with *Colchicum speciosum* 'Album'. It is of similar shape, with the rich purple diluted but continuing down the tube. At the RHS trials at Felbrigg Hall

Below left: *Colchicum speciosum* var. *bornmuelleri*
Below: *Colchicum speciosum* 'Album'

Above: *Colchicum speciosum* 'Benton End'   **Opposite:** *Colchicum speciosum* 'Atrorubens'

in Norfolk, *Colchicum speciosum* 'Benton End' ('Cedric's Darkest') was slightly lighter – just one shade lighter on the RHS Colour Chart – but with a particular sheen and slightly fuller segments that made it distinct, but otherwise of very similar habit.

Colchicum speciosum 'Maximum'

The description by E A Bowles of this variety may not fit the plant of today, which is a strong rose-purple and quite late-flowering. He seemed to find increase rather

slow, but that isn't the author's experience with this old Irish selection. Here it produces masses of concolourous flowers on only medium-length tubes from every corm, which stand well for a good period.

Colchicum speciosum 'Rubrum'

This looks like a slim *Colchicum speciosum* 'Atrorubens', flowering quite late in the season and inclined to remain chalice-shaped, even in sunlight, when the sheen is seen at its best.

Above: *Colchicum* 'Autumn Queen' and *Colchicum byzantium*

Cultivars of unknown origin, mainly hybrids

Colchicum 'Antares'

This Dutch plant has pale pink segments which appear quite white internally, but with purple tips. It is of medium size and sounds better than it actually looks in reality.

Colchicum 'Autumn Queen' ('Princess Astrid') AGM ♈

'Autumn Queen' is usually the first of the large-flowered colchicum forms to flower. Look for the buds in mid-August in some years and by late August even in years of drought. The scented, mid-purple flowers are tessellated on a white background, with a pronounced white throat.

Colchicum 'Beaconsfield'

This has a light purple, tessellated flower, composed of quite narrow, slightly curled segments. The segments when viewed from the side are straight-sided, rather like the capital 'Y'.

Colchicum 'Conquest' ('Glory of Heemstede')

A distinct selection with two names: *Colchicum* 'Conquest' seems to be the one in vogue at present. This is a quite heavily tessellated, rich purple flower with a clear narrow purple edge to each segment. It was a Zocher and Co selection of about 1905. *Colchicum* 'Glory of Heemstede' had a number of entries in the RHS trial of colchicums at Felbrigg Hall; each proved to

Above: *Colchicum* 'Conquest'

misappropriated and the selection seems to be lost to cultivation.

Colchicum 'Dandaels'

One of the old Zocher and Co selections with globular flowers of pale lilac, which makes it very distinctive. Only on the inside is any tessellation apparent. The tube is creamy-yellow and does not show any pink or purple as it ages.

Colchicum 'Darwin'

One of the last species to flower, it is often well into October before these medium-sized, globular, deep purple flowers are to be seen. It was a selection made by Mr R O Backhouse of Herefordshire. This variety is slow to increase and is becoming increasingly

rare. The neat foliage is very late in emerging, often towards the end of March before it breaks ground level, by which time other colchicum leaves are well developed.

Colchicum 'Dick Trotter'

A large, late, pinky-purple flowering selection, with an attractive, almost metallic sheen. The perianth segments are paddle-shaped, with the white central line stopping well short of the tip. It is often found lingering into November, with its conspicuous greeny-white throat covering half of the inner segments. This was found in the orchard at Brin near Inverness, the home and garden of Dick Trotter, a gardener inspired by E A Bowles. It seems likely that *Colchicum speciosum* 'Album' was one of the parents.

Above: *Colchicum* 'Glory of Threave'

Colchicum 'E A Bowles'

It was inevitable that a colchicum should be named after this eminent gardener. This selection came from the peach-house border at Myddleton House, Enfield, London, and was grown and distributed by Dick Trotter. Overall, a dark shiny purple with a prominent greenish-white star in the throat. The anthers are white and the tube quite a dark pink. It is halfway in size between *Colchicum* 'Huxley' and *Colchicum speciosum* 'Maximum'.

Colchicum 'Giant'. (*C.* 'The Giant')

The nursery of Zocher and Co raised many seedling colchicums in the early years of the 21st century, of which many came about as a result of crossing *Colchicum giganteum* with *Colchicum bornmuelleri*. *Colchicum* 'Giant', was one of these selections and, as its name suggests, it is a tall pale-looking flower which is slightly tessellated and held on a creamy-white tube.

Colchicum 'Glory of Threave'

A selection from the Scottish garden of Threave House near Dumfries. It was once confused with *Colchicum* 'E A Bowles'. It appears in October and has dark purple flowers with a distinct sheen. The flowers are cup-shaped and by the time the plant reaches maturity, the stem has darkened to match the flowers.

Colchicum 'Harlequin' (C. 'Harlekijn')

A bicoloured flower, with the top of each segment creamy-white and the base a pinky-purple. Some colchicums, if under stress because of very dry ground or a stone above the flower tube, can appear white but usually return to normal the following season. In this 1988 introduction, the unusual colour combination is permanent, making it a truly distinct introduction.

Colchicum speciosum 'Huxley'

This is a large-flowered selection with broad, quite open segments of deep rosy-lilac, with only the faintest tessellation. The white throat marking takes about a third of the inner segment to gradually diffuse into pink. There is also a very slim but long white central line running through all these colour changes. This was another introduction by Mr R O Backhouse in the 1930s, who is probably more famous for selections of lilies, daffodils and snowdrops from his home at Sutton Court in Herefordshire.

Colchicum 'Lilac Wonder'

This ubiquitous selection is a uniform rosy-purple with pointed segments, each with a pronounced central crease running the full length. The white style has a small hook at its tip. It is prone to falling over in the first puff of wind but is very prolific with its flowers, even flowering satisfactorily on a windowsill.

Left: *Colchicum 'Huxley'*

Above: *Colchicum* 'Pink Goblet'

Opposite: *Colchicum* 'Rosy Dawn'

Colchicum 'Pink Goblet' AGM ♀

This fine, aptly named selection originally came from the garden of Dick Trotter, who broadcast seed from *Colchicum speciosum* 'Album' regularly in one spot, from which he selected this and also the plant that we now know as *Colchicum* 'Dick Trotter'. The very distinct, goblet-shaped flowers are really quite a pale pink, over even paler pink tubes. They are quite tall and look rather fragile, but are actually quite tough.

Colchicum 'Rosy Dawn' AGM ♀

A seedling from Barr and Sons, a nursery that ceased trading in the middle of the 20th century, with bright rose, chequered flowers with white centres. When the flower is freshly open and viewed from above, the inner three segments seem to form a triangle. It has become widely grown but is often encountered with other names attached. though any doubt regarding the naming can easily be checked at the first flowering.

Opposite: *Colchicum* 'William Dykes'　　　　**Above:** *Colchicum* 'Water Lily'

Colchicum 'Violet Queen'
One of the darkest forms, strongly tessellated purple-violet with a white throat and stem. The segments are narrower than many, with a conspicuous white central channel and a contrasting purple style. Another Zocher and Co plant that is widely available today.

Colchicum 'Water Lily' AGM ♀
A large double-flowered hybrid said to be between *Colchicum speciosum* 'Album' and *Colchicum autumnale* 'Alboplenum'. The many-petalled flower is a rosy-lilac colour and does resemble a water lily. It tends to flop, but as the head is large and quite compact, the effect en masse is quite pleasing. A Dutch selection from Zocher and Co.

Colchicum 'William Dykes'. (*Colchicum* 'Intermediate Dykes')
A free-flowering selection said to be from the same seedbed that produced *C.* 'Lilac Wonder'. The segments are a pale lilac colour with slight tessellation and are quite pointed. The pale tube darkens as it ascends and matches the flower where it widens.

Historically there were many more colchicum selections. For instance, the *Colchicum* 'Disraeli' painted for a book called *The Collins Guide to Bulbs*, published in 1961, bears little relation to the colchicum that is around today under that name. It seems that the cultivars have become very muddled, and although many mistakes have been rectified by recent RHS trials in the United Kingdom, the results have not yet filtered down to all the outlets. If some old colchicum cultivars have died out, there are always new ones to take their place and, in any case, perhaps the constitutions of the failed species were poor, so are best looked upon as having been merely transient.

Misnaming has given the large-flowered colchicums a negative reputation, so surely it is in the interests of all producers and gardeners to get it right. There are some new cultivars available which need evaluation, and it might cloud the issue further if we went down the same road as we did with the naming of snowdrops; but then it also might focus attention on a neglected genus and encourage more interest.

The smaller species

The smaller colchicum species are, with a few exceptions, best grown under cold glass or in pots. This ensures they can be given a fairly dry rest in summer and not be too wet in winter. Besides, some have small flowers which would be lost in an open border. These are not always easy to acquire and seed may be the best source of stock. Colchicums are generally slow from seed, being quite erratic in germination unless the seed is fresh, so do keep the seed pan for a few years to ensure all possible stock is gleaned.

The small-flowered colchicums are best accommodated in the deeper Long Tom pots or in bulb frames, where the corms can spread without constriction. Although the corm may have room in the pot, it is best to knock them out each year to check for those small but very damaging slugs that live between the corm and the tunic, weakening the plant by chewing holes in the corm and emerging at night to feed on the flower and leaves. In daylight they are hard to find, so a visit to the greenhouse after dark with a torch and tweezers is required. Seed is often set by these species, but can easily be missed when the dry leaves are removed in summer. The capsule is often at ground level, with the brown seeds hidden even deeper. Remove these before they become lost. Sow immediately so they will germinate in spring.

Colchicum alpinum
This is a small version of *Colchicum autumnale*, of a rosy-purple colour, from the high mountain pastures of central Europe. It has small segments to 3cm by 1cm (1¼in by ½in),

with two or three leaves after flowering. It has not been an easy plant in cultivation, being rather shy to flower.

Colchicum balansae
A plain flower varying from white to rosy-purple, which in good light has a very short stem. The segments do not overlap, but are quite a feature, up to 7cm (3in) long. The corm can develop a long tube to 50cm (20in), requiring deep planting in a bulb frame. The leaves are absent at flowering time, and eventually grow 30cm (12in) long by 7cm (3in) wide. Found in Turkey and Rhodes.

Colchicum baytopiorum
This fairly recently described species from western Turkey is currently responding well to cultivation. The bright pinky-purple flowers, measuring some 4cm (1½in) across, are produced, unusually, with quite short leaves in mid-autumn. Although reputed to be tender, this species has survived for six years in an unheated frame, flowering well each year. However, the temperatures have not been particularly low in the recent past and the test may be yet to come.

Colchicum boissieri
From the eastern end of the Mediterranean, southern Greece and south-western Turkey, this species has rhizomatous corms, rather like a large wood anemone. The flowers are freely produced, up to 5cm (2in) in diameter and a bright rosy-lilac on quite short tubes. They are untessellated but have a white central line extending from the base, and prominent yellow anthers. They do need space and are best in a large pan, rather than

Above: *Colchicum boissieri*

a pot. If this species is planted in a bulb frame it tends to invade adjacent baskets (if grown in a frame), making retrieval quite difficult.

Colchicum corsicum

Closely related to *Colchicum autumnale*, this Corsican species can also be cultivated in the open. The pink and white flowered forms seem to be produced in equal numbers.

Colchicum cupanii

This species is widespread; it can be found from south-eastern France eastward to Greece and Crete and even in North Africa. A variable species, untessellated pink to a rich purple. Some forms have stripes running the length of each segment, giving a candy-stripe appearance, while others remain cup-shaped, never becoming star-shaped. The flowers are only up to 3cm (1 in) across, but make up for their lack of size by their sheer number. The two to three leaves are present at flowering. *Colchicum cousturieri* seems to be simply an island variation of *Colchicum cupanii* and well within the range found on mainland Europe.

Above: *Colchicum cupanii*

Colchicum lingulatum

An early autumn flower, 3–4cm (1¼–1½in) across and usually plain pink in colour with non-overlapping segments. The anthers are yellow and the distinctive broad (2cm [¾in] wide) glaucous leaves with blunt ends follow later. *Colchicum lingulatum* is best grown under glass because it does need a dry summer rest, coming as it does from north-western Turkey and Greece.

Colchicum micranthum

A small species from Turkey, with pale pink, often nearly white flowers 2cm (¾in) tall. In a pot this little corm produces a succession of flowers early in the autumn, with three to five narrow shiny green leaves growing later. They need strong light to open fully.

Colchicum parlatoris

This is similar to *Colchicum pusillum* in that it has up to ten narrow leaves which are produced after flowering. The flower is a darker purple-pink and of shorter stature and more star-shaped, with yellow anthers. It requires frame or pot cultivation.

Colchicum parnassicum

Allied to *Colchicum autumnale*, but with a finer corm tunic, arching leaves and quite short-stemmed pink flowers that last well in the autumn weather. They are best in pots, but could be tried in a sunny raised bed.

Colchicum psaridis

This species is from southern Greece, flowering in mid-autumn, from elongated rhizomatous-like corms. The flowers are rather open-segmented, pale purple-pink, occasionally white with contrasting nearly black anthers. Another feature is the presence of the two or three narrow leaves at flowering time. Like *Colchicum boissieri*, the roving habit is best contained in a pot, rather than a basket.

Colchicum pusillum
This species is quickly identified by the presence of up to six narrow (2mm [1⁄16in]) leaves which are produced at flowering time or soon afterwards. The starry, pale pink to white flowers can be 6cm (2½in) across and have quite narrow long segments. This plant is found in Crete, Greece and Cyprus.

Colchicum sfikasianum
A relatively newly named endemic species from the Malea peninsula, in south-eastern Greece. The pale pink, starry flowers are usually subtly chequered. It has yellow anthers. The three or four leaves follow the next spring. Best grown in a pot under glass.

Colchicum stevenii
More robust than many of the smaller species, this plant does well in a sunny raised bed where the bright, plain, rose-purple flowers are freely produced. The segments do not overlap, but are large enough to make an impact, with the numerous channelled leaves emerging at the same time. Found on Cyprus and Mediterranean lands to the east.

Colchicum troodii
The true plant has rich pink to white flowers produced in succession from quite a large corm. Many narrow, slightly hairy leaves follow, with the plant thriving under glass, as long as the old flowers are removed to avoid botrytis spreading from the dying flowers to the corm. From similar locations to *Colchicum stevenii*, but definitely suited to pot cultivation.

Colchicum turcicum
Selections are grown with striking reddish-purple flowers, up to 6cm (2½in) in diameter, which may be the *Colchicum atropupureum* of gardens. There are paler pink options available, so either buy in flower, or better still grow from seed, as they do vary. Although quite large it seems to dwindle in the open garden and is best grown under glass. The leaves of *Colchicum turcicum* are slightly twisted and ascending, to a length of up to 15cm (6in). This plant is found in the Balkans and north-western Turkey.

Colchicum umbrosum
A small-flowered plant with almost hooded, pale pink, nearly white, flowers, some 5cm (2in) long, which eventually open to a star. The segments can also be of unequal length and precede the strap-like leaves, which reach to 15cm (6in). From the Caucasus and northern Turkey.

Colchicum variegatum
A spectacularly tessellated flower of some size, with a star-shaped, widely opening flower to 5cm (2in), with the base of each segment overlapping. The anthers are purple and held on long filaments. The leaves that follow are greyish green and wavy-edged. This plant is easy to cultivate under glass, and hails from dry rocky places situated around the Aegean Sea.

Crinum

A bulbous genus from Asia and South and Central Africa, some of which have adapted well to cultivation in the northern hemisphere. They are all large bulbs and need very large containers or sheltered borders to flower at their best. Most often grown is the hybrid *C. x powellii*, which is hardier than either of its parents. All the bulbs are shaped like huge onions with long necks and need planting with the top of the neck visible. Once planted they are best left undisturbed for many years, as root constriction seems to induce flowering. In times of severe frost they benefit from a covering of straw or fleece. The old leaves need clearing in spring as they can stay fused to the new growth and look unsightly. If new stock is required, lift the bulbs in spring and replant in enriched soil. This is an undertaking that needs care, as the bulbs are always well embedded and deep, so treat like a shrub, initially digging away from the bulbs and then under to release them without damage.

Crinum x *powellii* (*C.* x *powellii* 'Roseum') AGM ♀

This hybrid between *Crinum moorei* and *Crinum bulbispermum* flowers from July into September, unlike the parents, which are only summer-flowering. The plant needs full sun to flower well and then the 1m (3ft) tall, stout stems can hold an umbel of up to ten pink trumpet-shaped flowers some 12cm (5in) long. The large-channelled, almost succulent leaves are long and do need exclusive space, or they will smother smaller plants. There are a few named selections of some antiquity which are hard to locate, but are still available from specialist nurseries.

Crinum x *powellii* 'Album' AGM ♀

A Victorian first registered in 1888, with pure white flowers and just as hardy as the type. The plant always appears just a little smaller, but is very effective against a dark background.

Crinum x *powellii* 'Harlemense'

This soft pink-flowered form, with large umbels, came from the Dutch firm of E H Krelage and Son in 1919. It is still listed today.

Crinum x *powellii* 'Krelagei'

This is from the early part of the 20th century and is very large in all its parts with deep rose-pink scented flowers.

Crinum variabile

A shorter species which has grown and flowered well for some three years in an open, but sheltered part of the garden. The flower stem is 60cm (24in) tall with pale pink flowers in the usual umbel. The foliage is quite glaucous and much shorter than *Crinum* x *powellii*. It flowers from late summer into autumn.

Above: *Crinum x powellii* 'Album' (Chrysalis Image Library)
Below: *Crinum x powellii* (Chrysalis Image Library)

Crocus

Crocuses are without doubt one of the highlights of autumn: reliable and easily cultivated, with most autumnal species thriving in the open garden. Many will set seed in a temperate climate and build into attractive colonies in just a few years. One or two flowers can look rather forlorn, but careful siting to suit their cultural requirements will speed multiplication. There are candidates for full sun, part shade, damp shade and some will even take to short grassland with aplomb.

It is to be regretted that the terms 'Autumn Crocus' and 'Meadow Saffron' were ever applied to autumn-flowering colchicums, as they still confuse many general gardeners and, more worryingly, some horticultural writers. Some gardening mail-order catalogues still headline their autumn colchicum section as 'Autumn Crocus', which does not help the true autumn crocus to become more popular and well-known. Writing in a similar vein, E A Bowles in *A Handbook of Crocus and Colchicum for Gardeners* points out that 'The presence of the six stamens is sufficient in itself to distinguish a Colchicum from a Crocus.' [crocuses have three]. Admittedly both are corms, but the storage organs are very different, with crocus corms always having a tunic composed of fibres, distinct to each species. These tunics provide a very useful guide and in some cases are the identifying feature that defines a species.

Many autumn crocuses look best in drifts, either in borders among small perennials or on their own to give the garden a marvellous highlight as other plants wane. Others can be planted in grass, which will need to be kept short through until late summer and not cut again until early the following summer as the crocus leaves wither. The seeds ripen in spring and can be left to naturalize and increase, or can be collected and sown in late summer in pans for greater control. The seed pods begin life at ground level and as they ripen are lifted clear of the ground. In some, such as *Crocus kotschyanus,* the pod can be 5cm (2in) above the soil, whereas others, such as *Crocus banaticus*, always seem to nestle just above the ground. These are easily overlooked and may need collecting with stout tweezers as the seeds begin to scatter.

Left and opposite: *Crocus niveus*

Crocuses can also be extremely easily accommodated in pots or a bulb frame. Their small stature means that many can be grown in a relatively small area, and they can give a display from August until the very end of autumn. If you grow these crocuses in frames and greenhouses the intricate markings and the full display, from tightly closed spears to fully open goblets, can always be seen. In the garden the individual flowers may not be in pristine condition, but this does not matter as in this sort of planting the whole view is more important. The cultural treatment of your crocuses will naturally match their garden position, which in turn depends upon their location in the wild. One added bonus of pot cultivation is the protection from the elements it affords, both for plant and gardener. It also means that the more tricky subjects can be specifically cared for and the vital pollination undertaken artificially and not left to a roaming bee. To this end a pair of tweezers is essential in order to remove an anther and deliberately brush any ripe stigmata of the same species. I have even heard of gardeners posting anthers to other growers so very rare crocus stock can be increased in different collections.

Crocus aleppicus

This first species is rare and only for bulb frame or pot cultivation, where a period of dry rest can be assured in summer. It is a plant from the countries adjacent to the eastern Mediterranean seaboard, found in mountainous areas as well as sand hills near the sea where summers are very dry and hot. It may also be a little tender and need protection from severe frost, but over the last

few winters has done well in a cold house in a deep sand plunge. The flowers are usually white, certainly on the inside of the segments, with quite variable markings of purple suffusion on the outside. They are not large – just 2cm (¾in) long – and occur with the very narrow leaves, which lengthen later. The flowering coincides with very low light levels at the end of autumn, so maximum exposure to all daylight is needed to stop the flower etiolating excessively.

Crocus asumaniae

This southern Turkish crocus has only been in cultivation since the 1970s. It has a restricted distribution on the north side of the Taurus Mountains. It seems to grow best in a bulb frame or pot, where some dryness can be assured in summer. In cultivation it flowers reliably in mid-autumn and has no foibles, increasing well. The flowers are white or pale lilac, with a pale yellow throat, and are usually surrounded by five or six barely emerging leaves. These are grey-green and quite narrow.

Crocus autranii

A rare species both in the wild and in cultivation. It occurs in alpine meadows in the Caucasus and in cultivation requires a situation that never dries out. Rather like *Crocus banaticus,* it needs a humus-rich but well-drained medium for pot-growing. It may prosper in the open garden, but as yet there does not seem to be enough stock to experiment. The flower is quite extraordinary: bicoloured segments with violet tops and white bases. The leaves appear much later, the following spring.

Above: *Crocus biflorus melantherus*

Crocus banaticus AGM♧

This meadowland crocus, hailing from Romania, has a unique flower construction, looking more like a small lilac iris than a crocus, which led to the discredited name *Crocus iridiflorus*. A uniformly coloured flower with large outer segments surrounding the three smaller erect inner ones. The stigmata are finely branched, of a similar colour and over-top the flower. The leaves are quite broad and do not develop until well into spring. Some variants have been named: there is the pure white 'John Marr', 'Rosamond', a pale lilac form, and 'President', a large deep purple, the last two from the Victorian gardener James Allen of Shepton Mallet, Somerset, who was better known for his snowdrop collection. It needs a cool position, but is easily grown in short grass, shady borders and rock gardens, as well as making a fine display in a humus-rich compost when pot-grown. It will regularly set seed and build into a long-lasting colony.

Crocus biflorus melantherus

This subspecies from southern Greece is the only *Crocus biflorus* to flower in autumn. The background colour is white with external purple veining; occasionally the markings become much more suffuse and almost a brown shade. Very noticeable are the black anthers, which are variable, and it is worth choosing those with strong colour. Just to confuse, a very few have no black marking and the anthers are the usual yellow, a feature more pronounced as the flowers age. The flowers are of quite short stature and seem to do best with frame or pot cultivation, flowering in October, by which time the leaves are just beginning to grow.

Crocus boryi

A creamy-white flower with some feathering of brown on the outside, produced with the dark green leaves in mid-autumn. The throat is yellow and the anthers white. A widespread crocus in Greece and Crete, found over basic as well as calcareous rock and quite variable to the gardener's eye. There are some very attractive goblet-shaped forms that produce many flowers from one corm, as well as different feathering patterns that make selection important. It is still a species for the frame or pot, but does seem perfectly hardy. Occasionally the feathered forms can look very close to *Crocus laevigatus* and it may require the corm tunic to be checked to see if it is papery and not hard and crusty as *Crocus laevigatus*.

Crocus cambessedesii

This is a small but very attractive crocus from the Balearic Islands, best suited to frame or pot cultivation because of its size. In flower it can vary considerably, from white to a mid-lilac, with the three outer segments delicately striped with purple. The leaves accompany the flowers, which usually begin in September, but they can be somewhat staccato in their production.

Crocus cancellatus cancellatus (C. cancellatus var. cilicicus)

The most common subspecies was commercially known as var. *cilicicus* and is a very attractive light blue with a strong violet striping. It is a good October garden performer, increasing particularly in well-drained soil. The plant is from southern Turkey.

Opposite: *Crocus boryi*
Right: *Crocus cancellatus cancellatus*

Above: *Crocus cancellatus mazziaricus*

Crocus cancellatus damascenus

This selection comes from the most easterly point of the species range and is described as coming from the hills around Damascus. This is a dry and rather hot region, so consequently the corms need a definite rest in summer and are best in a frame or pot. The flower is often very pale lilac with violet veining, similar in fact to the previous subspecies, except for the very coarse netted corm tunic which even forms a ruff at the base of the perianth tube.

Crocus cancellatus lycicus

This plant is from the Antalya province of Turkey. It differs essentially in that its leaves are quite well-developed at flowering and pale, nearly white flowers without veining, but a contrasting yellow throat and lolling, bright orange stigmata.

Crocus cancellatus mazziaricus

A mostly Greek plant, widespread but with a very scattered distribution, flowering nakedly in October. The flowers can be quite large and pale to deep lilac with dark veining. It will tolerate a sunny raised bed but thrives in drier frame conditions.

Crocus cancellatus pamphylicus

This Turkish plant is easily identified by its white anthers, rather than the yellow of all the other subspecies. The flower is white with a very noticeable yellow throat and only very faint veining.

Crocus cartwrightianus

This beautiful form of saffron crocus makes a very showy display, as, unusually, once the flowers have opened they stay open until they wither. They have broad segments of purple with darker veining, with some having a dark purple mark at the base of the segment. In the wild and in cultivation there are many stunning albino selections, which highlight the red style and yellow anthers. There is still a selection called *Crocus cartwrightianus albus* in cultivation that is really a pure white form of *Crocus hadriaticus*. It is soon identified by the more pointed segments than the white forms of *Crocus cartwrightianus. Crocus cartwrightianus* is probably the link with the wild form of the saffron crocus of commerce, which is unknown in the wild and also sterile. The corms thrive in a frame, but will also do well in a sunny raised bed.

Below: *Crocus cartwrightiamus*

Crocus caspius

A very attractive crocus, with quite large flowers, produced in ones or twos, sometimes white, otherwise a pinkish-lilac with a yellow throat. It comes from Iran, to the south of the Caspian Sea. It does well under glass and may yet prove to do so in a raised bed. It is slow to increase and needs regular seedlings coming on to supplement the stock.

Crocus gilanicus

This is a small species, only recently described. It can be very easily overlooked when grown with more colourful cousins. It is whitish, with near-white anthers and yellow stigmata all held within the flower. Despite this rather drab description, it has delicacy and interest especially if the form grown has some faint purple lines. It seems best cultivated in a frame or pot. It was named in 1973 from material found in northern Iran.

Crocus goulimyi

This is one of the gems of autumn crocus. Only known since the 1950s, this southern Greek species has proved to be a strong garden crocus, long-lived and increasing well. It is found only in the south-east of the Peloponnese, where it is locally abundant, usually at quite low altitude. The flowers are fairly uniform in colour, mauve to a rich purple, with the smaller inner segments often just a shade paler. As with many plants there are albinos: one was selected from a seedbed in the Netherlands and named *Crocus goulimyi* 'Mani White'. It is a vigorous and attractive selection, just as reliable in cultivation.

Below and opposite page: *Crocus goulimyi*

Crocus goulimyi leucanthus

This is only found in a very isolated colony and was only recognized in the latter part of the 20th century and given subspecies status. It is mostly an impure white, but does contain a few pinky-lilac plants. All the selections set seed regularly in cultivation, despite the radical difference in climate.

Crocus hadriaticus

Another species restricted to southern Greece, where it stands out from other white species by virtue of its bright orangy-red stigmata, as it is allied to the saffron crocus. The white segments can have variable amounts of brown or purple staining spreading up from the base. There are lilac and pure white forms found in Greece, which may become fixed as subspecies. The often-used name 'chrysobelonicus' is unsustainable in the light of modern knowledge and best left unused. This is a species best grown in a frame where protection can be provided.

Crocus hermoneus

A rare plant from Israel and Jordan, similar to *Crocus cancellatus*, but without the coarse tunic around the corm. The flowers are lilac with purple striping. It needs a dry rest in summer to succeed and then is not such a good garden plant as *Crocus cancellatus*.

Right: *Crocus goulimyi leucanthus*
Opposite top: *Crocus hadriaticus* in the wild
Opposite bottom: *Crocus hadriaticus* in cultivation

Above: *Crocus hyemalis*

Crocus hyemalis

This crocus helps to fill the late autumn gap by flowering in November. It is reputed to be tender, but has been outside in a well-drained, sunny scree bed in my garden for over ten years without any ill effect. If starting from seed it would be prudent to keep some stock under glass, to make sure it is amenable to your conditions. The flowers are produced with well-developed leaves. They are usually white with some purple marking at the base and they have blackish anthers. This is a common crocus in Israel and deserves to be better known in cultivation.

Crocus karduchorum

A. plant rare in cultivation – and often the name is misapplied. There was some confusion with the original collection, which has unfortunately been perpetuated for many years, with *Crocus kotschyanus* var. *leucopharynx* serving in its place. The true plant has the same strange, lopsided corm as *Crocus kotschyanus*, and a lilac flower, but has delicate, dark veining fading into the white base and very attractive, much-branched, white stigmata. It should do well in a raised bed, but initially it might be best to build stock under glass.

Crocus kotschyanus cappadocicus

This is the least-known subspecies of this important garden species. It has the misshaped corm and pale lilac flower typical of the species, which can have very attractive veining and only a small yellowing in the throat.

Crocus kotschyanus kotschyanus

An easily cultivated October-flowering crocus. It sets prolific amounts of seed and also produces offsets, so a good stand can soon be forthcoming. The flowers are lilac with a yellow throat and creamy-white anthers. It will grow in short grass, as well as most garden positions. The leaves begin to grow soon after flowering and do need some disguising; *Cyclamen coum* works well in this respect.

Opposite: *Crocus kotschyanus kotschyanus*

Crocus kotschyanus var. leucopharynx

Similar in all respects to the preceding entry, except that the throat is white, a fact only discernible when the flower is open.

Crocus kotschyanus suworowianus

This is one of the first crocuses to flower in late summer, often starting in August. It can be treated like the others, but seems a little slower and less inclined to set seed every year. This corm can be grown in a reasonably shady frame where the pots are never dried out and watered in late summer to initiate flowering. The flower is white with some purple veining and could be confused with *Crocus vallicola*, except there are no pointed tips to the segments.

Crocus laevigatus

Another stalwart garden flower for autumn, with selections flowering from October through to March. The species is found in Greece, many of the Greek islands and Crete. From this relatively small area the flowering time varies considerably, with the mainland Greek forms generally flowering in autumn. Even these vary considerably, with the inside of the flowers lilac, sometimes very pale and the exterior of the outer three segments silvery or buff, occasionally yellow. The form with yellow variation is extremely attractive, albeit rather small in stature. They are good garden crocuses, long-lasting, but probably need a raised bed to be appreciated, as they are one of the smaller crocus.

Below: *Crocus laevigatus*

Above: *Crocus medius*

Crocus longiflorus

This Italian species will thrive in a raised bed where drainage is good, and survives the vagaries of autumn weather very well, considering it can flower well into November in most seasons. The flowers vary from lilac to mid-purple with or without external darker veining. This veining used to give rise to varietal names (such as var. *melitensis*), but in the wild this is merely a range of variation, so these names are invalid.

Crocus mathewii

A recently described species from Turkey, named after Brian Mathew. In the type plant, the white segments have a rich purple throat and the stigmata is long and a prominent orangy-red. The white segments may be replaced by pale lilac and the purple area be smaller in extent, but in its most vivid form it is a stunning crocus. It flowers nakedly in October, with the leaves following immediately. It grows well under cold glass, but may also take to outdoor cultivation, when stocks allow experimentation.

Crocus medius

A very reliable performer for the open garden in October, as long as the soil is well drained. It is usually a rich purple with veins extending up from the throat, with a bright orangy-red, much-branched stigmata. It flowers nakedly and produces many cormlets to soon build into an effective feature.

The plant comes from a relatively small area of south-eastern France and north-western Italy, where there is considerable variation in colour. There is a selection in cultivation attributable to Oliver Wyatt, which is very prolific with its offsets, flowers well, but never seems to set viable seed. The usual stock behaves normally, regularly producing seed.

Crocus niveus

In its most attractive forms, *Crocus niveus* is a sumptuous flower, large and white or very pale lilac with a contrasting deep yellow throat. From the Peloponnese, this species is best grown under cold glass, although it thrives in a few favoured gardens.

Crocus nudiflorus

This species has long been cultivated in the UK, originally as a source of saffron, and has become naturalized in a number of counties, from Sussex to Cumbria. It is a tall crocus, usually of a deep purple, with the colour fading down the perianth tube. The leaves do not follow for some weeks after flowering and continue to grow throughout winter. The corm develops stolons and together with seed production a colony will often soon build, in short grassland or an ordinary border. This is really a crocus of the Pyrenees and its hinterland, where a few selections of albino corms have come into cultivation. *Crocus nudiflorus* 'Orla' is the modern selection. It has very beautiful, milky-white flowers with good vigour. It sets seed regularly, but as yet has not produced white progeny.

Crocus ochroleucus

This is one of the last autumn crocuses, flowering well into November in the open garden. It is a cream colour with a yellow throat and, if truth were told, not in the first division of stature, but when most other crocuses have finished flowering this deserves a place in every garden. The flowers rarely open wide in the low light levels of late autumn, which does give them some protection from the wind and rain. It will obviously do better under glass, but will even succeed naturalized in short grass. Native to Lebanon and northern Israel there are variations, one without the yellow throat, but as yet they are rare in cultivation.

Right: *Crocus nudiflorus* 'Orla'

Crocus oreocreticus

A plant from the mountains of Crete, allied to *Crocus cartwrightianus*. The purple flowers are distinctly darkly veined with a buff or silvery exterior which is still obvious when the flower is closed. The broad yellow anthers are topped by an orangy-red stigma, with the grey-green leaves just beginning to grow. *Crocus oreocreticus* is an easy plant to grow in a frame or pot, making a fine and eye-catching show.

Below: *Crocus pallasii*

Crocus pallasii

A widespread crocus found in south-east Europe and some parts of the Middle East. It flowers well when grown under glass, but is not as large or dramatically marked as some of the other 'saffron group'. The typically grown form is pale lilac with a three-branched red style, with the grey-green leaves growing soon after the flowers fade. In the subspecies *dispathaceus*, the segments are narrow and often a dark reddish-purple and the style is yellow. The effect is quite different to any other crocus – curious but engaging.

Above: *Crocus pulchellus*
Right: *Crocus robertianus*

Crocus pulchellus

The bowl-shaped, pale lavender flower has fine darker veins held on a slim perianth tube. The throat is white but still provides a clear contrast to the white anthers. There are some albino forms of equal beauty and like so many plants their seedlings unfortunately revert to the type colour, necessitating regular separation of corms as the only means of propagation. The annulate corm is small and very receptive to growing in the open garden.

Crocus robertianus

A large crocus from mainland Greece, with lilac-blue, substantial flowers some 15cm (5½in) in height. Its large, orange, frilled style adds to the beauty of the flower. It seems reluctant to increase vegetatively, but sets seed in cultivation. It is a valuable addition to a sunny raised bed and of course can be grown under glass, as long as it is not dried too much in summer.

Crocus sativus

Gardeners have only recently taken up cultivation of this sterile crocus, long farmed for its style branches, saffron. Not found in the wild, it is thought to be a historic selection of *Crocus cartwrightianus* which through centuries of vegetative reproduction and selection has lost the ability to produce seed. It can be reluctant to flower and needs regular splitting and deep planting in enriched soil to flower well. The flower is large and lilac-purple, with a long, lolling, red-orange stigma that protrudes beyond the segments.

Crocus scharojanii

This crocus is worth the little extra care it needs to maintain its flowering condition. It is the most attractive of the autumn species with yellow flowers. It is a damp-growing plant from meadows in and around the Caucasus and is best assured of similar growing conditions by growing in a pot or a designated damp humus-rich bed. A summer drying will not necessarily kill it, but flowers will not form and it seems hard to initiate the habit in succeeding years. The flowers appear early in autumn and the leaves many weeks later.

Crocus serotinus

The species has three subspecies, which differ considerably in their needs, so each will be considered separately.

Crocus serotinus clusii From the Iberian peninsula, this subspecies can vary in colour from pale to dark lilac, with the darkest forms usually treasured by growers. The naked flowers appear in October and thrive in a bulb frame or pot.

Above: *Crocus scharojanii*

Crocus serotinus salzmannii (Crocus asturicus) This has the same variation in colour but is a little taller with more pointed segments. It has a wide distribution from North Africa to northern Spain. This is a good crocus for the open sunny garden as long as the soil is well drained. Often the distinctly green leaves are present at flowering.

Crocus serotinus serotinus This Portuguese plant is the least cultivated of the three subspecies. The flowers again vary from pale to deep lilac in colour, with faint veining appearing on all segments. The corm tunic is more coarsely reticulated (netted) than the other two subspecies. It is best cultivated under glass.

Crocus speciosus AGM ♀

A very widely available and quite easily grown general garden crocus for autumn. It is found in Greece and eastwards as far as Iran. Many selections have been made and sustained as each corm produces many cormlets, making for assured distribution. It is a tall flower and can vary from a rich purple through lilac to white, with a prominent reddish-orange stigma and yellow anthers. The throat can vary from white to yellow. It usually flowers in September. The following selections are generally available each summer:

• 'Aitchisonii' A large plant with pale lavender-mauve, quite pointed segments.
• 'Albus' AGM ♀ A fine white form which holds its own in a mixed colony.
• 'Artabir' A 19th-century Dutch selection with light blue flowers and dark veins.
• 'Cassiope' A large flower of bluish-lavender, with a yellow base.
• 'Conqueror' A deep sky blue flower of considerable size.
• 'Oxonian' An English selection which to be truthful is not an Oxford blue, but a deep violet-blue, a colour which is continued down the perianth tube. A little slower than the others, but well worth acquiring.

Crocus thomasii

This species is related to *Crocus pallasii*, but looks a more substantial flower of usually deep lilac, with the green leaves present at flowering. It has a slim, reddish stigma and quite pointed segments. It does well under glass, flowering reliably in early October and consistently setting seed, a sure sign it is functioning well.

Crocus tournefortii

An island species from Greece. The lilac-blue flowers have contrasting feathered orangy-red stigma, which loll over the flat-faced flower. Once open they remain so until they wither. This feature is an attraction, but does leave them open to damage from heavy rain. So, although they can be grown in a raised sunny bed, they are best under glass. In Crete the flowers are much paler and in some areas seem to have hybridized with *Crocus boryi*.

Crocus vallicola

This is a damp-loving species that flowers very early, often in late August. Found in Turkey and adjacent land to the north-east, it is an easy plant to cultivate under glass or in the open garden, as long as the soil is humus-rich and never too dry. The white, sometimes purple-veined flowers have elongated tips to the segments. This makes them instantly differentiated from the similar *Crocus kotschyanus suworowianus*. It flowers nakedly and regularly sets seed. This is the most usual method of increasing stock, as few corms ever seem to increase vegetatively.

Crocus vitellinus

Rather like *Crocus laevigatus*, this species flowers at different times from late autumn to spring depending upon wild origin. It is orangy-yellow with some having a suffusion of brown-purple on the outside. The flower is quite slim and is accompanied by the fine leaves. It is best grown under cold glass.

Top right: *Crocus tournefortii*
Right: *Crocus vallicola*
Left: *Crocus speciosus* 'Oxonian'

Cyclamen

Even in the open garden it is possible to find at least one cyclamen in flower in every month of the year. In autumn there is even more choice, with cyclamens able to equal any spring display. Cyclamens are, as a rule, very undemanding plants that take to cultivation very well. Their positioning in the garden is really a matter of scale, with their ability to either multiply in colonies or to stay as discrete groups. For instance, *Cyclamen hederifolium* will in a relatively short time self-sow in whatever space you are prepared to allow. This largesse is not a vice, as there are few more arresting sights than sheets of this cyclamen in September. On the other hand, *Cyclamen intaminatum*, which flowers at a similar time, needs a much smaller, controlled garden site closer to the eye to do it justice.

Propagation is by seed, preferably sown as soon as ripe – usually the summer after flowering. This will ensure quick germination, matching the leaf growth of the parent. It is advisable to leave the seedlings in the pot for two growing seasons, before carefully teasing the roots and leaves apart and potting on. If the seed-growing medium is without soil, it is best to give the pot a few dilute liquid feeds when the plant is in growth.

In the garden, top-dress the area when the tubers are dormant with a little bone meal or equivalent included in sieved compost to shallowly cover the tubers, which naturally come to the surface. As with all storage organs each annual root extension will rarely be into new ground, so extra feed helps keep flowering performance.

Some of the autumn-flowering cyclamen species will need growing in pots; this may be because they are tender, such as *Cyclamen rohlfsianum* and *Cyclamen africanum*, or because they are quite small, so are better appreciated close to the eye. The pot-grown plants will all need particular care as the flowers fade, especially if the flower is unfertilized. The dank atmosphere of autumn allows botrytis to spread very easily and these flowers are prone to infection. This infected tissue will soon infect adjacent leaves and stems, causing serious damage to the health of the tuber. A pair of tweezers is an essential tool to aid removal of the spent flowers as soon as they fade. Coiled stems and seed capsules pull themselves inwards and although the threat of botrytis from the withered flowers is less, they are best teased out so the seed capsule can mature without any decaying petal attached.

In summer when the tubers are dormant, this is one of the first groups of plants to consider at bulb-potting time. June is not too early to begin the task of assessing the needs of each pot. There is no hard and fast rule, but removal of the compost as far as the tuber soon reveals its size and the state of the compost. Cyclamen do not need annual repotting; in fact many growers consider an annual feed and top-dressing to be the best way to encourage flowering. This process can be employed for a few years before obvious overcrowding dictates a larger pot and new compost. This is still best carried out in midsummer, so new roots delve well into the compost before winter. In any case there will often be a dip in the flowering performance after repotting.

Cyclamen africanum

This plant comes, as the name suggests, from North Africa, and often begins to flower in early autumn. It is very close to *Cyclamen hederifolium*, but when handled can be seen to generate leaves from a central boss, which ascend immediately, unlike *Cyclamen hederifolium* which spreads, then ascends. The roots develop from all over the tuber, again differing from *Cyclamen hederifolium* which has none beneath. It is seemingly tender, susceptible to wet rather than dry cold, so is best housed in a frame or greenhouse, where it can definitely be given a dry shady rest in early summer. There is some rather black humour which suggests the only way to be sure which species you have is to plant it out and if winter kills it, you have your answer – this is an approach not really to be recommended! The plant never seems to need much water: immersing the pot in water to half its depth for a short time just as growth begins seems adequate and then give it further watering around the edge of the pot throughout the growing season.

The pink, very occasionally white flowers have prominent auricles and develop with the leaves. The leaves are variable in shape, dark green with small amounts of marbling. They persist all winter and spring, dying down only as summer approaches. They are then best stored in a dry, warm spot such as under the benching in a greenhouse, where the compost is dry but not desiccated.

Left: *Cyclamen africanum*

Cyclamen cilicium AGM ♀

This species comes from the Cicilian Taurus in southern Turkey. It is a small plant, quite slow in developing, but well worth the effort. It can be pot-grown very easily, but equally is at home in an open site that may be sheltered but receives sun for much of the day. In this type of locality you do need to establish seedlings, as one plant looks insignificant; in time a group, with the typical neat pink flowers with darker carmine markings near the mouth, will perform well in mid-autumn.

Opposite: *Cyclamen cilicium*
Below: *Cyclamen cilicium* forma *album*

Until recently there were some very small, white-flowered forms available, which were very undistinguished. Now we have *Cyclamen cilicium* forma *album,* a pure white selection with quite large flowers that breeds true from seed. This is equally at home in the garden. All of these plants have quite small leaves that appear with the flowers. These leaves are spoon-shaped with a wavy margin and variable amounts of a pale margin forming a hastate pattern. The undersides are uniformly a reddish-purple. Like so many cyclamen they can live for many decades and even then the tubers will rarely be more than 8–10cm (3¼–4in) in diameter.

Cyclamen cyprium

Endemic to Cyprus, this is a tender, sweetly fragrant species of great beauty. The flowers are white with a small 'm' of carmine at the mouth. The petals are twisted and there are also prominent auricles. The flowers usually appear just before the leaves in September and are very durable, often surrounded by a ruff of leaves as autumn develops. The leaves themselves are quite small and sombre in patterning, with an olive green background with paler green blotches. There is a much more spectacularly marked form, *Cyclamen cyprium* E S, standing for Elizabeth Strangman, who used to run the sadly missed Washfield Nursery in Kent. This silver-splashed selection, which seems to come true from seed, came from the nursery in the 1960s. A plain, dark green-leaved form is also available.

This plant is best given the protection of a frost-free greenhouse, where it is almost worth growing for its scent alone. In maritime climates it has succeeded outdoors in a sheltered position. It needs a dry summer rest; however the odd light watering during summer to imitate a thunder storm seems to ensure autumnal growth starts on time. Occasionally they may remain dormant for a whole season; if this happens, simply check the tuber and if it is sound, plunge the pot under the staging and just keep it barely moist until next autumn when it will usually spring into life as expected.

Below and opposite: *Cyclamen cyprium*

Above: *Cyclamen graecum* subsp. *graecum* forma *album*
Opposite: *Cyclamen graecum*

Cyclamen graecum

This is a variable species from the eastern Mediterranean, Greece, some of the islands, Crete and south-western Turkey. This distribution has led to the recognition of three subspecies (*anatolicum*, *candicum* and *graecum*). The tuber is quite round, with the thick roots emerging as a bunch in the centre of the base. With age, the growth points lengthen to become floral trunks, making repotting a tricky undertaking.

The foliage and flowers appear at about the same time in September, peaking in October. The leaves show great variation in their patterning of cream to silver over a velvety-green background. The flowers vary from pale to dark pink, with three magenta veins at the base of the flower that can run halfway up each petal.

There is also a pure white-flowered selection, *Cyclamen graecum* subsp. *graecum* forma *album*. A very distinct feature of *Cyclamen graecum* is the seed pod and more particularly the way the peduncle (the old flower stem) coils. It coils only from the ground, leaving the stem next to the seed pod quite straight. This is a useful feature to help identification in the field.

Above: *Cyclamen graecum*

In cultivation a deep pot is necessary to accommodate the thong-like roots. The old custom of baking the tuber to induce flowering has been superseded by a gentle resting in a damp plunge. However they are still not regular performers in cultivation and it may be that some tubers will always flower more prolifically than others. It is well worth growing a number of plants and selecting the best, as a floriferous pan (shallow pot) of this plant is a highlight of autumn.

Cyclamen graecum subsp. *anatolicum.* (*C. cyprograecum*)

This form is from southern Turkey, northern Cyprus and Rhodes. The leaves are twisted and predominately green with a pale centre. The flower colour varies but has dark magenta blotches at the base on quite short stems.

Cyclamen graecum subsp. *candicum*

This form is from western Crete and has more pointed, quite dark green leaves with pale hastate patterning. The flowers are white to pale pink with a solid magenta basal blotch, which can extend well up the petal.

Cyclamen graecum subsp. *graecum*

This is mostly found on mainland Greece. The leaves are generally muted in colours of pale and dark green with a rough edge. The flowers are pink, although a pure white plant was found in the Peloponnese.

Right (top and bottom): *Cyclamen graecum*

Cyclamen hederifolium
(C. neapolitanum) AGM ♆

If only one autumn cyclamen is to be grown, then it must be this one. It is very accommodating, flourishing in so many garden situations, some quite unexpected. Ideally a semi-shaded site in friable (easily crumbled) soil suits it very well. Here it will self-sow profusely and soon build into a spectacular sight in early September. This is not a plant to grow singly; it looks best in patches or sweeps in the open garden or under deciduous trees. Once the flowers have finished, the leaves form a dense umbrella over the ground, and look attractive in their own right. They continue looking quite fresh until May. Then in June or July the leaves can be removed, seed pods collected and the site top-dressed and fed, with bone meal or similar. In July the first precocious flowers will emerge to start nearly ten months of display.

The recurved flowers of pink or white are large, with quite sharply pointed petals with conspicuous auricles. There is a double magenta-purple V-shaped mark at the base of the flower that fades into the petals. Scent is variable, but not usually very strong. The flowering period is very long, with some still seen in November. The leaves are, as the name suggests, of ivy shape, but they can be round, toothed, smooth and even pointed, with every pattern imaginable on the upper surface. There are selections that are plain, others all silver and some distinctly ringed with silver. One of the joys of this plant is the infinite variety produced, giving the gardener the chance to select their favourite.

Right: *Cyclamen hederifolium*

The tubers can equal the human expectation of life and can expand to dinner-plate size, quite flat-topped and rooting from the sides and top, but not from beneath. In nature the tubers often sit on the soil surface and can become detached, so a top dressing helps to keep all the roots attached and active. The flowers and foliage tend to spread sideways before rising, so a wide pot is necessary for the plant to look attractive. They soon outgrow pot culture, or at least a pot that is easily transported.

Cyclamen hederifolium is found from south-eastern France eastwards to western Turkey in countries bordering the Mediterranean Sea, including many of the islands. With such a wide distribution, variation has evolved and selections and varieties have been collected and named. *Cyclamen hederifolium* var. *confusum* is found in the centre of its range, in locations quite close to the sea, such as Sicily, Crete and the southern Peloponnese. The leaves are large, shiny and thicker than usual, with less obvious patterns. They seem to be found in dense shade, where the flowers come nakedly with the leaves appearing soon after. Despite its maritime locations, it seems just as hardy, but appears to need good light to flower well some 20° further north.

There are many selections of *Cyclamen hederifolium* available, but because they are seed-produced, no two are exactly alike.

Below: *Cyclamen hederifolium* var. *confusum*

Above: *Cyclamen hederifolium* 'Nettleton Silver'

Sometimes there is a close resemblance to a named form and there is always the chance of finding an improved form. At least any selection and removal of inferior stock is an easy operation with cyclamen.

Cyclamen hederifolium 'Nettleton Silver', 'Silver Cloud'

These and other silver-leaved selections are widely available in garden centres and nurseries. They seem to produce a high percentage of offspring with silver leaves, and any inferior seedlings are easily removed to keep the colony looking uniform. There are the usual white and pink flowers. The pink flowers are often pale, so any really dark pink seedlings do make a stunning contrast and are worth marking for subsequent seed collection. The leaves can suffer from botrytis and any that have been affected in this way are best pinched out and destroyed. There are many named forms and selections available, which are probably best chosen in flower and leaf to be sure they are really different from the huge range that soon occurs in any garden as stocks build.

Cyclamen intaminatum

This is the smallest of all cyclamen, with near-circular leaves of plain green or with a slight marbling. The flowers are white or pale pink with a distinct grey veining and no basal blotch. It was only given specific status in 1988.

Cyclamen mirabile

A species from western Turkey that is similar to *Cyclamen cilicium*. The leaves differ in being rounded and toothed, and in selected forms pink or even red on the upper surface. As the leaves age, this colour fades but is sufficiently long-lasting to make this plant very attractive. The plant is easily grown in a cold frame or greenhouse, but like *Cyclamen cilicium* can be grown in a special place in the garden, where other planting provides a little shelter but does not overhang the site in autumn. The flowers vary from pale to deep pink and are very neat, tapering to a small nose with a magenta mark. In addition, the petals usually have a serrated margin. There is a pure albino form, but this is very rare.

This plant, almost more than any other cyclamen, requires the grower to sow all his fresh seed and in due course prick them out into trays, to grow on for one more year. Then subjective selection of the leaf form and colour can take place; by then a few will even be flowering. The best can be potted and the rest planted out to form a significant display in early autumn.

Cyclamen purpurascens AGM ♀

This species is rather an enigma. It grows further north than any other, so one would assume it would be easy to accommodate in northern gardens. It certainly grows, but rarely seems to flower profusely. In fact it will often sulk, maintaining its leaves for much of the year and sending up a few flowers from summer until well into autumn. As it is relatively small and takes little space, it is worth experimenting in semi-shaded niches with young tubers to see if a successful position can be found. This species is from the mountains of central Europe, found in moist deciduous and coniferous woodland.

Although this plant was awarded an AGM, it must have been more in expectation than reality. There are some attractive leaf designs and shapes becoming available, but they do not have the same impact as *Cyclamen hederifolium*. The plain-leaved Fatra form from Slovakia does seem to flower more readily in cultivation. Seed is not abundantly produced so should be gleaned wherever possible.

Cyclamen rohlfsianum

An African species from Libya, where it grows in limestone gullies in the typical terra-rossa soil. After *Cyclamen africanum*, this is often next to flower, usually nakedly at first, but soon followed by large expanding leaves. The sweetly scented flowers have a distinctive protruding stamen cone, rather like Dodecatheon flowers. They need a frost-free environment and careful watering to succeed.

The tubers, once established, grow quite quickly into knobbly, large, often concave shapes. This makes watering a tricky business, as it is essential to keep water from rotting the tuber. In August lower the pot into water to dampen the compost sufficiently, but keep the tuber dry. The plant does not ever seem to need much water and should be kept quite dry once the leaves have withered. A resting position beneath the greenhouse bench seems to suit its requirements. It seems to flower best after a sunny warm summer, but whatever the weather should always be in a light sunny position once growth begins, with plenty of room to accommodate the canopy of developing leaves.

Above: *Cyclamen mirabile*

Cypella

These bulbous plants are from Mexico southwards to Argentina, usually found in meadowlands where the soil never dries out completely. The flowers are ephemeral, but are produced over a long period, with many making their season of interest from late summer into autumn. The flowers look superficially similar to iris, but with three large spreading segments and three far smaller recurved ones in the centre.

The leaves of this member of the Iridaceae are quite narrow and deeply pleated. Seed is usually set. This seed is quite large and easily collected from the elongated capsules. Most are best grown in the cool greenhouse, where water can be reduced in winter and then increased as the days lengthen.

Cypella coelestris (C. plumbea)
This is a large plant to 70cm (28in) with correspondingly large flowers to 8cm (3¼in) across. They are effectively blue, as the name would suggest, with a suffusion of brown with yellow markings near the centre. The leaves are iris-like, up to 2cm (¾in) wide. It requires frost-free growing in winter, but can be planted out to flower from July until September in a sunny position and then lifted and stored as dry bulbs during the winter. Alternatively, the pot could be placed in the border with the pot itself concealed beneath the soil, or displayed in the usual way until frost threatens.

Cypella herbertii
This is the hardiest species; in fact in my own garden it has thrived in a sunny bed for over a decade without any extra protection and has even formed a small colony by self-sowing. The flowers are a bright yellow some 5–6cm (2–2½in) across, with some browny-purple marking centrally. It can reach 50cm (20in), but is usually a little less. The plant flowers for many weeks, sometimes well into October, with older flowers already in seed at this stage. The leaves are slim, pleated and held below the flowers.

Cypella herrerae
An attractive plant with deep blue flowers with the inner, smaller segments forming a small crest of yellow. It flowers late in autumn and will need to be grown in a cool greenhouse and exposed to as high a light level as possible. The leaves are quite short and can produce bulbils in the axils. Culturally the plant should never dry out, particularly in summer, when it can happily reside in a plunge exposed to the rainfall of summer.

Eucomis

A South African genus of almost succulent-leaved bulbs, which flower from summer into autumn. Increasingly more and more are succeeding outdoors, as long as they are deeply planted in well-drained conditions exposed to full sun. They have suffered from

Opposite: *Eucomis autumnale*

mistaken naming. However, with seed of species being available directly from South Africa, as well as new, well-illustrated books, this problem is slowly being resolved. There are many hybrids available, which are superb garden plants, but some initially came into commerce as unidentified species. Now in Britain these are given cultivar names, so the attractive bulbs, often quite colourfully flowered, can properly take their place in gardens. They have the common name of Pineapple Lily, a very apt name as each flower is topped by a bunch of leafy bracts, reminiscent of a pineapple.

Eucomis autumnale

This species has very obvious, fresh green, strap-shaped leaves, which have undulate margins and extend to 45cm (18in), with a flower spike to 30cm (12in). The raceme is whitish or pale green, fading to a darker shade. In the subspecies *clavata* the stem is half as tall, but the flowers are still as large.

Eucomis bicolor

A taller stem to 60cm (24in), often purple-spotted. The flowers have purple margins to the white petals. The slightly undulate leaves are quite broad and do tend to flop as they mature. This plant requires moisture in summer to flower well.

Eucomis comosa

The flower spike can reach 1m (3ft) in well-grown specimens, but is usually less. The stems are spotted purple, with very variably

coloured flowers, which can range from white to near red, all with purple ovaries. The raceme is large and can take the upper 30cm (12in) of the stem; unfortunately it causes the stem to flop over as the plant matures. The leaves can be green, or purple in some selections. Common to all is the much-reduced pineapple tuft at the stem top.

Eucomis pallidiflora (E. punctata var. concolor) AGM ♀

A very statuesque plant with a substantial raceme of greeny-white flowers to 75cm (30in). The green, quite broad leaves have very tight, wavy margins. A reliable plant for a sunny, damp border.

Eucomis pole-evansii

The tallest eucomis, reaching 1.8m (6ft) when growing well, with wide leaves to 60cm (24in) in length. The long raceme has wide-opening, green flowers covering a third of the stem. This could be a vigorous form of *Eucomis pallidiflora*.

Eucomis schijffii

A high altitude species from the Drakensberg mountains. The stem reaches 20cm (8in) or less, with a wide, flat pineapple tuft. The flowers are predominately purple and held just above the leaves. In the northern hemisphere it flowers in July through to September. The broad leaves are short and, although green, reflect some of the purple hue of the stem. This plant is relatively new to cultivation, but should prove to be hardy.

Right: *Eucomis zambesiaca*

Eucomis zambesiaca

A choice, hardy, white-flowered plant that seems to thrive in drier areas and still flower well and regularly. The stem can be as much as 30cm (12in), but it is usually less, with apple-green leaves and pineapple tuft. The plant flowers in August and September, and in warm autumns seed is usually set. This plant is at its best in early autumn and does well in a sunny position.

Galanthus

When considering snowdrops, their late winter flowers immediately come to mind. Indeed their colloquial name 'Fair Maids of February' is very apt. There are some species and forms, however, that flower from mid-autumn onwards. The species most associated with autumn is *Galanthus reginae-olgae* from Greece. This plant was named in honour of Queen Olga of Greece, the present Duke of Edinburgh's grandmother.

There has been a proliferation of snowdrop cultivars named in the recent past, with a few flowering in autumn. The selection and naming of these plants seems to have been quite arbitrary, but at least with the recently published monograph on snowdrops, by Matt Bishop et al, there is now a basis for comparison and merit. With the light levels of autumn dropping day by day, the planting site is an important factor if the bulbs are to thrive and multiply. All snowdrops grow in southerly latitudes, some as snow-melt plants and others in deciduous woodland, where they receive very good light intensity combined with moisture. In more temperate climates this translates to well-drained but moisture-retentive conditions, in good light. Planting in evergreen shade will etiolate the flower stems and, equally, fast drainage where drought is prevalent will result in poor growth. This still leaves many positions in alkaline and acidic soil conditions where they will thrive,

particularly under deciduous canopies. Some, in fact, work best in sunny sites, with a minority requiring pot or frame cultivation to succeed.

There is an ongoing debate about the merits of lifting and dividing just after flowering, as opposed to lifting as dormant bulbs in summer. Both work, as long as care and a few basic steps are followed. For cultivated stock the lifting 'in the green' is fine as long as the roots stay moist and are replanted very quickly in well-prepared soil enriched with some humus. Moving and replanting dormant bulbs works just as well as long as they do not become desiccated. If they are to be kept out of the ground for any length of time, they need storing in virtually dry sand or vermiculite and have to be planted as soon as possible. The recent bad press regarding dry bulbs comes from the imported wild collected bulbs, usually from Turkey, which are lifted 'in the green' in late winter, dried off in shaded sheds in Turkey, and shipped across Europe to end their days in a box or in airy bags surrounded by shavings, for sale in the UK in late summer and autumn. The chances of these bulbs, which have been out of the ground for at least six months, ever beginning to grow are quite slim. At the height of this trade millions of snowdrops were being imported each year; now numbers are more regulated, but there is still a worryingly high level of waste.

It is important to keep good stock pure. If a plant sets seed, the resulting seedling will be different and only rarely of a better form. So collect the yellowing seed pods before they dehisce and either sow immediately in a new area or better still in a pan of seed compost.

Opposite: *Galanthus elwesii* Hiemalis Group 'Barnes'

Self-sown seedlings are very common in gardens that are close to beehives. Even in autumn and winter on sunny days bees will take short flights to snowdrops and fertilize at random, leading to quite large amounts of seed being set. This random progeny is the delight of galanthophiles looking for new forms, but the very devil in corrupting named stock.

Galanthus cilicicus

This is a relatively unknown snowdrop, which needs either careful siting or pot cultivation to thrive. It will grow well in sheltered niches, such as under eaves protected from the north, but is best kept in a frame until stock increases, allowing for some experimentation. This plant, hailing from the Cilician Taurus in Turkey, has been known for over a hundred years, but is still rare in collections. It has slim, grey, glaucous, flat leaves, which tend to recurve at the tips when mature. The flowers look like those of the common snowdrop, but are produced in November and December. This species seems to prefer an alkaline compost and a dryish, cool rest in summer.

Galanthus elwesii
(Galanthus caucasicus)

For many years gardeners happily identified snowdrops using both these names, until *Galanthus caucasicus* was shown to be virtually unknown in cultivation. In consequence of this finding, all autumnal selections are now included as forms of *Galanthus elwesii*. There are many different selections in gardens, some with rather thin segments and poor markings. The list below is an attempt to select a few that have some additional

features other than that of flowering early. These plants all have their leaves exposed to the vagaries of winter and can become damaged by spring, so inspection is needed to see if any damage is leading to fungal infection before natural decay occurs. If discolouring of the leaves is apparent, apply fungicide to prevent the spread of any infection. Alternatively, lift the group, discard any suspect bulbs and replant in fresh soil.

These selections seem to flower best in sunny positions that are protected from the wind. The bulbs are relatively small, with corresponding small flowers and leaves, unlike their spring cousins which are usually larger in all respects.

Galanthus elwesii 'Athenae'

This November-flowering snowdrop comes from Broadleigh Gardens, Somerset. It is very susceptible to the weather conditions: in the 2002–2003 season the display was excellent, but in the previous year growth was stunted. The leaves are barely formed at flowering and the sinus marking is pale green, with a broad and rounded 'V' and the flowers have a broader look to them than the Hiemalis Group flowering at this time.

Galanthus elwesii Hiemalis Group 'Barnes'

This plant was brought from Barrs Nursery in 1928 and given by the Northampton surgeon E B Barnes to O E P Wyatt, who noted it was an early 'caucasicus', sometimes flowering by the end of October. Today 'Barnes' is just as early, but is appreciated for its quite substantial rounded outer segments as well as the glaucous, broad leaves.

Galanthus elwesii Hiemalis Group 'Don Sims' Early'

A prolific selection distributed by the late Don Sims from stock given to him by Sir Fredrick Stern's gardener. Like all plants at this time of year, they last in flower for many weeks, soon forming eye-catching groups in full sun. The flowers are quite narrow but long, with the usual small 'V' marking.

Galanthus elwesii Hiemalis Group 'Earliest of All'

Another late autumn selection from Wyatt, generally a little later than 'Barnes' and with narrower outer segments and a thin inverted 'V' marking.

Galanthus elwesii Hiemalis Group 'Harold Wheeler'

A new find from Gloucestershire with a much darker green ovary and 'V' marking. Equally early-flowering and easy to please.

There are many other plants in cultivation that are best simply given the name *Galanthus elwesii* Hiemalis Group, as they are narrow segmented with a pale marking. They are very reliable garden snowdrops, but any selection in this area does need to be judged against those that already have been named.

Galanthus elwesii 'Peter Gatehouse'

A late-autumn flowerer with a short pedicel held tightly into the spathe. The upright flower is surrounded by short leaves, which

Right: *Galanthus reginae-olgae*

elongate later and are quite narrow and glaucous by the new year. The flowers are quite distinct with an elongated green 'X' on the inner segment.

Galanthus elwesii 'Remember Remember'

This hybrid is usually in flower by early November. It is of good substance with a large dark green apical mark that covers half the inner segment fading towards the ovary. The leaves are only just emerging at flowering and as the flower is held on a long scape, it does need a sheltered site to remain vertical for long. Still a very choice plant and well worth accommodating.

Galanthus peshmenii

A recently named species from Turkey. For many years the island form from Kastellorhizo was grown as the 'Turkish *Galanthus reginae-olgae*'. It has also been found inland in the adjacent Antalya province. The leaves have a distinctly greenish hue, with a faint, pale central channel, and generally they are shorter and less robust than *Galanthus reginae-olgae*. It grows easily in a frame or pot, flowering without leaves in October. In the open garden, trying to mimic its habitat seems to be the best option: try placing it in a well-drained niche between two rocks. The flowers have pale bridge markings which are reflected in the colour of the ovary. Seed seems to be freely set and the bulbs quickly form bulblets around the basal plate, so the plant should easily be maintained in cultivation.

Galanthus reginae-olgae

This species has been known for well over a hundred years and is well established in cultivation. As with many Victorian plants there was a proliferation of names for plants which all turned out to be *Galanthus reginae-olgae*. The last name to fall was *Galanthus corcyrensis*, a form found on Corfu and in Albania which has quite well-developed leaves at flowering time. The usual Greek plants flower without leaves, which follow immediately after flowering. However this distinction is hard to maintain as more plants are grown with such a variety of leaf development observed at flowering time.

This species is found in specific habitats where hot summers are ameliorated by aspect or by the nearness of perennial water, usually under a deciduous tree canopy, thus ensuring good light intensity when the leaves are above ground. The plant has typical snowdrop flowers very similar to the common snowdrop, but the leaves are very distinct with a central glaucous stripe and by spring can reach some 25cm (10in) in length. This species does well in pot or frame cultivation, where seed is regularly set. It can thrive in sunny well-drained locations, such as those found beneath deciduous trees or in raised beds. It seems to be quite a gross feeder, so to maintain flowering, benefits from a feed, such as bone meal, once a year.

This species is usually the first snowdrop to flower in autumn and is therefore particularly treasured by gardeners, who have made numerous selections, some very distinct.

Opposite: *Galanthus reginae-olgae*

There is scope for new and distinct cultivars to be named, especially as seed is set so regularly. The outer segments are sometimes marked with green striping, which could lead to some selections that could be given cultivar names.

Galanthus reginae-olgae 'Cambridge'
This came from the Cambridge University Botanic Garden, where it had been growing for 40 years, originating from a collection from Corfu, Greece. It has substantial flowers with thick, ridged outer segments and a well-marked bridge on the inner. Recently some stocks of *Galanthus reginae-olgae* 'Cambridge' have been proving harder to maintain – this is a real shame because it is a fine plant.

Galanthus reginae-olgae 'Hyde Lodge'
A very tall cultivar originally given to Dr Mackenzie, who runs the Giant Snowdrop Company in Gloucestershire, by Herbert Ransom. The flowers are of good substance, rounded and ridged. The inner segment bridge marking is broken in two.

Galanthus reginae-olgae 'Tilebarn Jamie'
Named by Peter Moore, who is usually more associated with cyclamen, but here has selected a fine vigorous cultivar, which often produces two scapes per bulb. The flowers have outer segments that are very waisted where they join the ovary, giving them an appearance of small butterflies.

Opposite: *Galanthus reginae-olgae 'Tilebarn Jamie'*

Gladiolus

A few of the South African gladiolus flower in late summer and autumn. These cormous plants from the south-western Cape region usually start into growth in autumn as the rains begin and then flower in spring, but a few flower more quickly, making use of the light and the residual heat of autumn. These corms are best in a cool greenhouse where they are planted in late summer in a well-drained sandy compost. The autumn-flowering varieties should be in good light and encouraged to grow on into late spring to build up the bulbs for the next year.

Gladiolus carmineus
The flowering stem reaches to 30cm (12in) and has a one-sided spike of large deep pink or carmine red flowers. The long grass-like glaucous leaves follow after flowering. This is a sea-cliff plant from the southern Cape.

Gladiolus maculatus
A tall species to 70cm (28in) with up to four strongly fragrant flowers per stem. They are cream, blotched with brown or maroon. The slim green leaves are of equal length. This is a widespread plant of mountainsides.

Gladiolus sempervirens
This species grows further east than the others and receives some rain all year. It is evergreen and flowers in late summer into autumn. There are many large red flowers on a one-sided spike. It may be nearly hardy and worth trying outside in a sheltered position. It grows in damp locations up to 1700m (5580ft).

Habranthus

A small genus, mostly from temperate South America. They are barely hardy, although, as they are prolific seeders and flower quickly from seed, it is worth experimenting with sheltered sites in the open garden. Certainly *Habranthus tubispathus (Habranthus andersonii)* can survive for many years in a well-drained scree, flowering regularly, then disappearing only to reappear nearby in a year or so. In pots of sandy loam they are very easy and accommodating to grow under cold glass. They usually have just one flower per scape, which is held around 45° from the horizontal, unlike zephyranthes which are generally held erect. To be certain about the subtle differences that separate the two genera you need to look at the stamens. If they are of two different lengths they are habranthus, but if all the same length, they are zephyranthes.

Habranthus brachyandrus
Each 30cm (12in) stem has one large pink flower with a purple base. It has the narrow, strap-like, semi-succulent leaves typical of the genus. It flowers in early autumn and if dried off in early winter can withstand some frost in the ensuing months.

Habranthus gracilifolius
A tall plant to 45cm (18in) with, unusually, near-cylindrical shiny leaves. The flowers, unusually more than one to a scape, are just over 5cm (2in) long, white or pink and sheathed by a green tube.

Habranthus martinezii
A pale pink flower with a darker base, freely produced in autumn. It will easily set seed and produce a fine colony in a frame, as long as there is a dry rest period in summer.

Habranthus robustus
The large pink trumpet-shaped flowers held on 30cm (12in) stems are produced in late summer and early autumn. It flowers before the fleshy leaves appear. It is not completely hardy, or it may be that it demands a dry rest in summer, as it does very well under cold glass. An easy and most attractive plant, which can be timed to flower by the first autumnal soaking two to three weeks before the desired event.

Habranthus tubispathus (H. andersonii)
The most commonly grown habranthus and one of the most reliable and easily grown. It flowers over a long period in early autumn, without the leaves which grow soon afterwards. The funnel-shaped flowers can vary from yellow to almost a copper colour and are about 3cm (1¼in) long, held on 15cm (6in) stems. There are a number of named varieties including *Habranthus tubispathus* var. *texanus* which is yellow and has naturalized in parts of Texas. The plant sets copious amounts of seed, which obligingly hang in their capsules for weeks on end, so aiding busy gardeners.

Opposite: *Leucojum autumnale*

Hippeastrum

All of the smaller-flowered hippeastrums have now been moved to the genus Rhodophiala, leaving only the tender species and hybrids intact. The large-flowered hybrids of now obscure origins are available from late summer and can easily be potted and induced into flowering by late autumn.

There are some smaller-flowered selections coming from the Netherlands which increase the available choice. Perceived wisdom says these bulbs need a minimum temperature of 5°C (41°F) when dormant, but they also seem to cope quite happily with an 'environment which is simply frost-free, and flower well the following autumn.

Leucojum

The snowflakes are a neglected genus in comparison with the snowdrops. True, there are few named selections, unlike snowdrops, but they have great diversity of form and many are reliable flowering plants for autumn. They come from Europe and North Africa and are all dormant in summer. The autumn-flowering leucojums have smaller flowers, with the leaves growing soon after flowering and lasting well into late spring.

Leucojum autumnale
An easily grown species, with a wide distribution from the Iberian peninsula, Sardinia, Sicily and North Africa. This has led to differences in stem colour, seed production,

Above: *Leucojum autumnale* in a raised bed

bulb division and the development of leaves at flowering, but basically they are all excellent small bulbs for a sunny well-drained position.

Up to four white pendant, bell-shaped flowers are held on 15cm (6in) stems, but often less. In some forms the white is tinged with pink, particularly towards the ovary. The leaves soon follow and are narrow and filiform reaching 15cm (6in) at maturity.

Leucojum roseum

A very beautiful pink-flowered bulb, rather like a diminutive form of *Leucojum autumnale*. As it is found in Corsica and Sardinia it may be a little tender, so is best appreciated in an alpine house. Pot in a free-draining, sandy compost and always attend to the pot in July, as the first flowers emerge in August. The single flowers soon set seed; in fact early flowers have ripe seed as the last flowers are fading. As vegetative increase is slow, this seed is the best way to build stock. It will often germinate that same autumn. It has thin greyish-green leaves which are produced immediately after flowering, which last right through the winter.

Leucojum valentinum

This species from central Spain and, most strangely, Greece is not common in cultivation. It grows to 20cm (8in), with a thicker stem and wider greyish-green leaves. The milk-white flowers, up to three per stem, are broadly shouldered and 1.5cm (¾in) long. It flowers quite late in autumn and can do well in some sheltered gardens, but is probably best in a pot, kept fairly dry but not arid in summer.

Lilium

This huge genus essentially contains summer-flowering bulbs of the first order. However there are significant numbers that only begin to flower as the days shorten, some even saving their peak until October and lasting into November. These stunning bulbs are often considered worthy of precious pot space, which enables the gardener to match the needs of the lily to the type of compost. Whether in a pot or in the garden, preparation of a large space is needed to allow the plant to show its full potential and build up a bulb for the following year.

All lilies like rich living, with plenty of humus and regular feeding. They respond amazingly to liquid feed, with young seed-grown bulbs flowering in their third year, if given regular waterings of the fertilizers used to feed tomatoes. These later-flowering lilies can be caught by frost, so siting is important, as is the ability to move heavy pots if frost is forecast. Ideally lilies need the treatment described in that oft-quoted maxim: 'Head in the sun, feet in the shade'. Lilies do not have any protective membrane to the bulbs and must never dry out, so full sun under a south-facing wall is not an option. However, a well-prepared bay within a shrubbery that has sun for half the day is an ideal site, as is a deep container that is shaded by a low wall or plants.

Another good use of lilies, which demands less attention, is to sink a container (usually plastic) of lilies in a border to bring colour at the end of the year just where it is needed. This eases the watering requirements and lessens the temperature fluctuations at the roots. Some of the later-flowering lilies are a little tender, so keeping them potted makes protection easier when frost threatens.

All the autumnal lilies need deep planting, with the soil well prepared and aerated. Humus should be added and a layer of sharp sand included as a base for the bulbs. It is helpful to pour sand in and around the bulbs to fill all the gaps left between the scales. These gaps make perfect homes for keeled slugs. Some lilies are said to require an acidic growing medium, but most simply need humus and moisture to thrive, and failure that is attributed to incorrect pH values is probably due to poor soil structure. Lilies that are not lime-tolerant can be planted in ericaceous compost to which lime-free grit has been added to aid drainage and then given appropriate liquid feed during the growing season.

One unfortunate drawback with lilies is their susceptibility to virus, which eventually so distorts the foliage that removal and burning is the only option. The best solution is to grow stock from seed, which means the new plants are free of infection at the start of their life. In order to minimize infection, always buy clean, undamaged bulbs that are fresh-looking, avoiding those desiccated specimens stored in bags of wood shavings that are offered for sale in some establishments.

Lilium auratum

This Japanese lily needs deep planting as it is a stem-rooting species. The stem reaches to 1.5m (5ft) with up to 12 large, bowl-shaped flowers, with recurved petals which are usually white with a prominent gold band. There are many variations, some with crimson speckling. All have scattered dark green lance-shaped leaves. It is hardy, but does need copious water during the growing season. It flowers in August and September.

Lilium formosanum

As the name suggests, this is a lily from Taiwan, where it grows from sea level to over 3000m (11,500ft). This naturally has led to many variations in height, hardiness and even time of flowering. It is very easily and quickly raised from seed, even flowering in ideal conditions within one year. The plant is not long lived, but this is not a drawback, given the speed at which it matures. The lower-altitude forms are taller and, given a sheltered site, seem to do quite well for a few

years. The stem can reach 2m (6ft), with numerous quite narrow dark green leaves. The scented, trumpet-shaped flowers are white with recurved tips, up to 20cm (8in) long. Externally there is some reddish-purple marking, which is more pronounced in the shorter forms. The taller forms flower later in the year; in some autumns flowers can still be found in late October.

Lilium henryi

A vigorous plant which forms underground bulbils with such profusion that the clump will need lifting every few years to maintain its flowering potential. It can reach 3m (10ft) but is usually much less, with lanceolate leaves changing to short and broad around the flowers. The flowers are a deep orange Turk's-Cap type held on long horizontal pedicels. It is an easily grown lily which will thrive in all but the most acidic soil. The flowering period for this hardy lily is from August into September.

Lilium lancifolium (L. tigrinum)

Better known to gardeners under the old name, this easily grown orange Turk's Cap can reach 1.5m (5ft), but is often shorter. It is sterile and does suffer from virus, so stock needs to be carefully watched and any with damaged brown leaves removed. It forms aerial bulbils, but these unfortunately transmit the virus. A strong bulb can produce up to 40 hanging flowers and although it is said to need acidic conditions, it has grown quite satisfactorily in a soil on the limey side of neutral.

Lilium speciosum

There are some doubts about the hardiness of this lily, so ample drainage in an acidic medium is essential to see it through the winter. Some ericaceous composts are very water-retentive and need added drainage material to prevent the medium becoming stagnant. If this is provided, this widely available lily will give marvellous value throughout the autumn.

The stem grows to just over 1m (3ft) tall and has scattered lanceolate leaves and a broad cluster of outward-facing or hanging Turk's-Cap flowers. These flowers can be white or pink with a much darker pink centre, with very prominent filaments and anthers.

Lilium superbum

A tall American lily, up to 3m (10ft) in optimum conditions of well-drained acidic loam in part shade. The leaves are in whorls and topped by orangy-red Turk's Cap flowers spotted with purple, some 7cm (2¾in) across.

Left: *Lilium formosanum*

Merendera

A small genus of corms that has many affinities with colchicums, and indeed is sometimes so named. However, merenderas are easily differentiated from colchicums by the gap in the perianth segments at the base of the tube. They are both autumn and spring-flowering.

The plants are all quite small and therefore need to be grown in raised beds or pots to be fully appreciated. The autumnal ones, particularly *Merendera montana,* are among the first of the truly 'autumnal bulbs', emerging from still-dry pots to catch out the unprepared gardener in late August.

Merendera attica
A narrow, star-shaped flower 3–4cm (1¼–1⅓in) in diameter, pale pink in colour, produced at ground level. *Merendera attica* can very easily be damaged by the weather, so is best cultivated under glass. The leaves form at the same time as the flowers. This plant is native to Greece and western Turkey, at quite low altitudes.

Merendera filifolia
The corm is small and dark brown with a long neck and does need extra care when repotting to avoid damage. This plant needs frame or pot cultivation to ensure a summer rest period, then narrow rose-pink flowers to 5cm (2in) across appear in September. It is possibly a little tender when grown in temperate climates, coming as it does from North Africa, southern France and the Balearic Islands.

Merendera montana
The best and largest autumn-flowering merendera species. Like the others the flowers open at ground level, but are larger, and in good forms, the red-purple flowers with white throats make a good show in late summer and early autumn. The flowering times vary, depending upon the provenance. The flowers are soon followed by the dark green leaves, which form a rosette. A meadow plant from Spain, especially in the Pyrenees, and Portugal.

Muscari

This is essentially a spring-flowering genus, but one species has evolved to take advantage of the light and warmth of autumn to ensure successful pollination, and another is a selection that begins to flower in October.

Muscari aucheri 'Autumn Glory'
This is usually a spring-flowering Turkish bulb which would be outside the remit of this book. However in the 1950s Ron Ginns of Northamptonshire gave to plantsman Ray Cobb some *Muscari aucheri*, a few of which flowered in the autumn. Ray separated them from the rest and distributed them as *Muscari aucheri* 'Autumn Glory'. It has a strange habit of flowering in autumn, with the flowers lasting well into winter, when further flowers emerge to take the display into spring. The flowers are held in a dense raceme and are mid-blue, topped by a paler blue cluster. The leaves, just two or three, are deeply channelled and quite wide with a hooded apex.

Muscari parviflorum

A small plant from around the Mediterranean basin, found in rocky places. It is only suitable for pot cultivation. The 10-15cm (4–6in) spikes are quite sparsely clothed by light blue, cup-shaped bells. The leaves follow and are narrow and linear and quite lax. The bulbs seem to require to be congested to flower, therefore repotting is undertaken only every few years and then into a well-drained sandy compost.

Narcissus

There are a surprising number of autumn-flowering narcissus, most only suitable for cultivating under glass, where a summer rest can be assured. Most narcissus occur around the Mediterranean basin, including North Africa, from near sea level to quite high mountains, where they are snow-melt plants.

Some 50 years ago the late daffodil expert Douglas Blanchard crossed *Narcissus cantabricus* with *Narcissus romieuxii* and some of the resulting selections were named after fabrics. A number have stood the test of time and strangely, or deliberately, chosen because they flowered as autumn advances. *Narcissus* 'Nylon' is actually a group name for similar clones that flower in October, with cream *Narcissus bulbocodium*-like flowers, with a slight frill to the edge of the corona. *Narcissus* 'Taffeta' is widely available, and has quite large white flowers, which are produced with

Left: *Narcissus minor* 'Cedric Morris'

Above: *Narcissus serotinus*

surrounding leaves only, so the abundant flowers are well displayed. This follows *Narcissus* 'Nylon' and runs into November.

As the light and heat are gradually diminishing, all autumnal flowers last for a long time and these plants are no exception, with the odd bloom still around at Christmastime. *Narcissus* 'Jessamy' is pale yellow with a slightly rounded corona, making the flowers appear quite large, again flowering in November.

There are a number of species and hybrids of the *bulbocodium* type that flower in autumn. The North African plants seem to provide the greatest range. I hesitate to give names as these plants may well be natural as well as garden hybrids, judging by the great variety of form and colour that emerge every year from the sand-plunge around the pots of narcissus. This is always a rich source of seedlings, which seem to be in perfect scale and in character.

Narcissus elegans

A tall species to 35cm (14in) with typical broad grey leaves at flowering. The flowers are in contrast quite small, 3cm (1¼in) across with creamy-white, slightly recurved segments and a small corona of yellowish-green. It is a slightly variable species.

Narcissus minor 'Cedric Morris'

A late-flowering selection some 20cm (8in) tall from northern Spain. It will begin flowering in late November and a sunny spot seems to suit it best.

Narcissus serotinus

A common species, from quite low altitudes, with white flowers and a much reduced corona of yellow-orange. The crystalline white flowers, sometimes three to a stem are flattish and up to 4cm (1½in) in diameter. The narrow leaves follow flowering. In cultivation the bulbs need to have a dry summer and be left undisturbed for a number of years to become very congested before flowering with any regularity takes place.

Narcissus viridiflorus

As the name indicates, a green-flowered plant with pointed green petals 3cm (1¼in) in diameter and a very reduced corona 1mm (1⁄16in) high. The stem to 25cm (10in) can have up to five flower heads, more fascinating than beautiful. A warm summer and congested bulb development seems the best recipe for flowering in cultivation, to emulate the conditions of the western Mediterranean.

Below: *Narcissus* 'Taffeta'

Nerine

A genus of South African bulbs which are mostly autumn-flowering. They flower nakedly after a summer dry period and then produce leaves during winter and more particularly spring. Sometimes the damper northern-hemisphere climate means some leaves are still present as the flowers begin to emerge. These are best removed as their job is done and they do spoil the display. Perceived wisdom suggests that only *Nerine bowdenii* and its hybrids are at all hardy in temperate regions. However it is now worth gambling with many more, especially if a reserve is kept under glass. I have managed to grow at least four other species in sheltered sites for many years, where in the open garden the temperature has regularly dropped to -6°C (21°F) each winter.

The flowers of this member of the Amaryllidacae vary from red to the palest of pinks, with albinos not uncommon. Each flower has six swept-back segments, often wavy-edged, exposing long conspicuous stamens. The autumn-flowering species need a summer rest period, which can be quite drying as the bulbs are well protected from extremes by a very dense outer skin. The few evergreen plants must not be dried, but kept moist during summer before water is increased in the autumn. *Nerine sarniensis* is well known in all its colour forms as a cut flower, but is really too tender for most outdoor cultivation.

Cultivation in pots requires a free-draining compost with regular additions of a high-potash fertilizer in the growing season. They make ample roots and may look as if in need of repotting every year, but try to resist this as flowering is best with the roots restricted and feed applied. When repotting is necessary, make this genus one of the first in late summer, thereby avoiding damage to the long rather brittle roots. In a similar fashion they seem to flower better outside when there is some restriction to their spread, afforded by a wall or pathway. This also helps to keep the bulbs warmer as well as inducing more flower.

Nerine bowdenii

This is the most satisfactory species for growing outside in a temperate climate. There have been numerous selections named and then muddled since this bulb was first introduced in the early 20th century. There are some attractive forms available, however, and there is a resurgence of interest from the Netherlands in mass-market distribution, with specialist nurseries providing some of the older selections. The species is from the high KwaZulu-Natal Drakensberg and the midlands of the Eastern Cape in South Africa, where the climate is quite severe. The flowers are held on 60cm (24in) stems, with up to eight flowers on quite long pedicels forming an umbel. The strap-shaped leaves begin to grow with the first warm days of spring.

These bulbs are best planted in spring between flowering and leaf growth. If they are received as dry bulbs then pot up to ensure the roots gain a foothold before planting them in the open garden. They may make growth in the open garden, but this will be tenuous if the spring is cold and frosty.

Right: *Nerine bowdenii*

Nerine bowdenii 'Alba' is an old selection that is now widely available and seems to come in colours from pure white to a very pale pink. All, however, are very attractive. A pale pink selection is 'Stephanie'. 'Manina' flowers in late September and is a little darker. 'Hera', at its best in early October, is a dark pink and probably is a hybrid with *Nerine sarniensis*, but seems to have inherited the hardiness of *Nerine bowdenii*. The new Dutch selection 'Promivetta' is a mid-pink and seems to be of fairly short stature, and 'Albivetta' is a near-white selection. 'Pink Triumph' is a mid-pink with a darker central streak to the petals.

The older selections are sometimes muddled. However they are worth seeking out. The early-flowering 'Mark Fenwick' ('Fenwick's Variety') is a strong pink on a tall dark stem. 'Mollie Cowie' has a good pink flower of considerable height, and is easily identified by its variegated spring foliage. 'Wellsii' ('Quinton Wells') has dark pink flowers, which are crinkled and form a tighter umbel. There are others available, such as 'E B Anderson' and 'Praecox', which may be distinct selections, but seem to be just strong-growing forms of *Nerine bowdenii*.

In most summers fleshy seed is set which drops into established clumps of bulbs, immediately growing roots in autumn. It is very easy for named selections to be corrupted by mundane seedlings, which are then innocently passed on as a named form. The moral is to collect your seed before it falls and then grow on without using the name of the selection. There is always a

chance, a very small one, that you may have a unique and beautiful plant to name.

Nerine filamentosa

The name really helps in identifying this species, as the pink filaments are straight and long, making a very conspicuous feature, especially obvious as the segments are rolled back for half their length. The umbel has a flat-topped appearance with hairy pedicels, all features that soon differentiate this from similar small-flowered species. This plant is technically evergreen, but watering can be reduced significantly during winter, when the 2mm, thread-like leaves can be tidied and the pot fed.

Nerine filifolia

The 2mm (1/16in) wide leaves, which can reach 20cm (8in) in length, give this species its name. It is ideal for pot cultivation, with up to 15 very delicate and attractive mid-pink flowers held in umbels by mid-autumn. The pot soon becomes congested with bulbs, but resist repotting until flower production lessens. This is an evergreen species, but it may lose many of its leaves in winter, which is a good time to clear out the old thatch, loosen the top dressing and replace with some fertilizer and grit ready for new growth in spring.

Nerine humilis

This is one of the winter-growing species, which needs a dry summer rest and a light sunny position under frost-free glass in winter to do well. It has been suggested that this is really a winter-flowering form of

Left: *Nerine* 'Zeal Giant'

undulata. It is variable in leaf size and flower colour as it occurs over a wide area of the mountains of the Cape. The pink flowers are irregular in shape with very wavy margins, particularly in the upper half, and are produced in September and October in the northern hemisphere. The flowering stems vary from 15–30cm (6–12in) tall and the flowering umbels also vary in size.

Nerine krigei

This is best under cold glass, where the spirally twisted leaves produced in summer give rise to the common name 'Corkscrew Nerine'. The 30–45cm (12–18in) stem has an umbel of strong pink flowers, with a dark pink keel. It is not as dense as some and is very easily grown and quick to bulk up.

Nerine masoniorum

This performs very well in pots and can be attempted on a sheltered rock garden, when stocks allow. The foliage is very slim, 1mm (⅟₁₆in) by 20cm (8in), and the umbel consists of many bright pink wavy-edged flowers with a dark pink keel, held on 3cm (1¼in) hairy pedicels. It flowers in early autumn, surrounded by the old leaves of summer, which need tidying as the flower stems emerge.

Nerine pudica

This is a very choice winter-growing bulb that needs a dry summer, then a damp autumn and winter in good light for optimum flowering. The umbel is quite loose, with relatively large funnel-shaped flowers,

Right: *Nerine masoniorum*

and a pink central keel. It is very attractive and is held on 30cm (12in) stems, which are gradually surrounded by the angled leaves as autumn advances. flowering is well into autumn and as the temperatures are dropping, the flowers last for many weeks, making this a very useful and underrated nerine. It can take a slight frost, but not one severe enough to freeze the compost.

Nerine undulata (N. flexuosa)

In the wild this species is very variable or may well be composed of different species. In cultivation we seem to have a very stable selection, which is semi-evergreen in the open garden, depending upon the severity of the winter. In any case, the bulb seems to thrive and still flower well each autumn, and in temperate climates will go dormant during the summer. In the meantime, until the botanists have named this plant to their liking, *Nerine undulata* is a very apt name, as the quite large pink flowers are undulate and held on stems 40cm (16in) tall. The dark green strap-shaped leaves grow simultaneously and seem to provide the bulb with enough food before winter damage. The white selection, *Nerine undulata* 'Alba', is quite superb, a pure white and just as easy to grow. Plant in a sheltered sunny niche to make sure it thrives. These sheltered sunny niches are always in great demand, but this plant is well worth the space.

Nerine 'Zeal Giant'

Usually grown in a container, but proving to be quite hardy planted in a sheltered, south-facing position, down to -6°C (21°F).

Oxalis

A huge genus of which just a few are tuberous and flower in autumn. These few are very demure, attractive plants, unlike some, which are among the very worst of weeds, especially when introduced as aliens, such as *Oxalis pes-caprae*, which has invaded so many areas in the Mediterranean region. The species described in this book are from South America and South Africa.

Oxalis hirta

A tuberous species from the Cape Province of South Africa, requiring some protection from frost. The stem grows to 15cm (6in) in autumn, with quite large pinky-violet flowers in the leaf axils. *Oxalis hirta* 'Gothenberg' is a large-flowered selection. There are other coloured forms, including yellow and white in cultivation.

Oxalis lobata

A small, dark brown, woolly-coated tuber from Chile that produces many bright yellow, four-petalled flowers in mid-autumn. The whole plant is less than 5cm (2in) tall, with the flowers 2cm (¾in) in diameter and surrounded by the typical clover-like leaves. This plant is strange as it then produces a fresh set of leaves in spring before going dormant for the summer. It seems to be hardy, although used to be considered borderline. In pot or garden the dormancy should be gentle and not too drying or hot.

Opposite: *Nerine undulata 'Alba'*

Below: *Oxalis lobata*

Oxalis perdicaria

This may be the correct name for *Oxalis lobata*. Whether this is true or not, to the gardener there are two very different plants here, both well worth growing. The foliage of *Oxalis perdicaria* is a paler green and slightly larger, but the flowers are really so very different, a pale primrose-yellow and just a little larger. In Chile there is much more research work to be done on these autumn-flowering oxalis.

Oxalis purpurea (speciosa) 'Ken Aslet'

This selection of the variable *Oxalis purpurea* is widely available commercially and although hailing from the Cape Province of South Africa, seems quite hardy in temperate regions. It is very profuse with its offsets, so a pot is soon full of dark brown roots. Not a bad thing as flowering seems better when there is some constriction. Just the plant for lazy gardeners! After a summer's dormancy, the silky-grey trifoliate leaves emerge and are then topped by up to 4cm (1½in) pale yellow flowers. It is usually grown in pots, but will thrive and flower in a sunny scree without constriction.

There are certainly white and purple forms of this attractive plant in existence, but the concentration on the yellow seems to have removed them from the commercial market. This is a pity as the white selections – in particular, 'Bowles' White' commemorating another famous English gardener – are well worth growing.

Oxalis versicolor

A late autumn-flowering plant from South Africa, where it is nicknamed the Candy Cane. This name is very appropriate as the white flowers have a red edge which, as they unfurl in a spiral, resemble the traditional confectionery. The plant's tufted, well-protected bulbs are numerous but still probably need cold glass in order to thrive, because the narrow leaves are produced in late autumn and winter.

Pinellia

These tuberous-rooted plants from China and Japan are essentially summer-flowering, but one or two last well into autumn, given a modicum of shade. They are essentially small woodland aroids, with a quiet attraction and all of quite modest proportions.

Pinellia pedatisecta

The tallest species to 30cm (12in) with bold, pedate leaves and a slim, quite enveloping green spathe some 15cm (6in) long, and a yellow enclosed spadix. This lasts for weeks and weeks well into autumn. Seed is regularly produced, but the stem soon collapses, allowing the seed a quick dispersal.

Pinellia ternata

A much more delicate looking plant with tri-lobed leaves and a slim spathe of green or purple, which has a small hood at the apex.

Opposite: *Oxalis versicolor*

The narrow green spadix often just protrudes from the top of the spathe. Bulbils are produced at the base of the stem just above the ground. They will grow best in half-shade, but are very tolerant of conditions. Wherever they are grown they do need to be close to the eye, as the enjoyment is in the detail not the distant effect. They, like *Pinellia pedatisecta*, are very long-lasting, and continue to send up new spathes over a long period.

Pinellia tripartita

The leaves are tri-lobed and quite broad, with wavy edges. The flower stems reach 10cm (4in), usually with a pale green spathe of thick texture. Some forms have purple spathes. The filiform spadix is considerably longer than the spathe and can protrude by 10cm (4in).

Rhodophiala

A South American genus, once included in the very closely related hippeastrum, but which now occupies its own niche. It flowers from late summer into autumn and can be manipulated to flower earlier or later by temperature and watering regimes. In fact, in temperate climates they seem to flower at quite differing times each year. They have semi-permanent roots, so should never be dried too much, just rested during summer and only repotted when congestion is obvious.

They are best treated as pot or bulb-frame plants until stock is sufficient to experiment in the open garden. Certainly *Rhodophiala bifida* will grow well in a sunny position and others may well prove equally amenable.

Rhodophiala advena

This mostly Chilean species is quite hardy and reaches 50cm (20in), when growing well, with glaucous 5mm (¼in) wide linear leaves. The trumpet-shaped flowers are held horizontally, varying from red and pink to yellow.

Rhodophiala andicola

The violet-pink, 5cm (2in) long funnel-shaped flowers are held erect on 20cm (8in) stems. The flat glaucous leaves radiate to 20cm (8in). A plant from southern Chile, where it grows in volcanic soils in open grassland at the tree line.

Rhodophiala bagnoldii

A yellow flower, often stained red, to 5cm (2in) in length, held erect on 30cm- (12in-) long stems. The linear glaucous leaves reach 30cm (12in).

Rhodophiala bifida

This species is from Argentina and Uruguay, which, although occurring further north than many, does seem to be one of the most amenable to open ground cultivation. The bright red flowers point upwards, with the few linear slightly glaucous leaves attaining 30cm (12in).

Rhodophiala chilensis

A bulb from the coastal lowlands of Chile. The flared, trumpet-shaped flower varies from red to yellow, with many intermediate forms. The narrow, linear leaves coincide with flowering.

Opposite: *Rhodophiala advena*

Rhodophiala elwesii

A species that has been in cultivation for many years. The pale yellow, trumpet-shaped flowers have a red throat and are often held singly on stems to 40cm (16in), but usually less. Found in the fairly arid grasslands of Argentina.

Rhodophiala pratensis

A robust plant to 60cm (24in) with up to eight flowers of reddish-violet per umbel. The bright green leaves occur at flowering and are large, 45cm (18in) long and up to 12mm (in) wide. A plant of Chilean grassland.

Rhodophiala rhodolirion

A spectacular species with large trumpets, some 8cm (3in) in diameter held on short stems. These flowers can be white or pink, each with red flecking in the mouth. A plant from the high and dry steppe in Argentina and Chile, at up to 3500m (11,500ft).

Rhodophiala rosea

From the island of Chiloe, Chile, a bright red flower, often solitary. It is held horizontally on 15cm (6in) stems and accompanied by two–three narrowly linear glaucous leaves.

Schizostylis

A genus of just one species, *Schizostylis coccinea*, from a South African region of summer rainfall. However, the plant is very tolerant of a temperate climate and although the semi-evergreen foliage may be damaged in winter it soon recovers to flower well in

late summer and on into autumn. It appreciates a damp niche, where the quite questing rhizomes soon make a dense colony just below ground level.

The lance-shaped leaves reach 30cm (12in) or more, with large, red saucer-shaped flowers produced in succession. In cultivation selections from white through all shades of pink have been made.

Scilla

A widespread group of essentially spring-flowering blue bulbs. However a few are not blue and even fewer have taken to flowering in the autumn. The European and Asian species are hardy, but the North African bulbs need to be grown under cold glass to survive. All are of very easy culture, amenable to a variety of situations, but probably flowering best in sun.

Scilla autumnalis
A native to Britain, but widespread throughout Europe and Turkey. When the small raceme of purple-blue flowers appear in late summer, it is one of the first signs that autumn is about to begin. The flower spikes are held above a small rosette of narrow leaves and are prolific with seed production. In southerly latitudes the flowers seem more vibrant, often pinkish, with albinos regularly occurring.

Left: *Scilla autumnalis*
Right: *Scilla lingulatum*

Scilla lingulatum

A North African species that flowers in October from quite large bulbs which are best kept frost-free. The leaves begin to emerge with the flower stems, which reach 10cm (4in) or so with a cylindrical raceme of blue flowers. They make an attractive sight surrounded by the shiny lanceolate leaves, which continue to grow through winter and spring. In the variety *Scilla lingulatum* var. *ciliolatum* the edges of the leaves have a fine white indumentum and a glossier surface otherwise it is very similar. Once the leaves have died down, the pot is best rested and kept quite dry until late summer watering.

Scilla scilloides

A pink-flowering plant from south-east Asia that is a little taller than *Scilla autumnalis*, flowering a little later through into September. The narrow leaves appear first, soon followed by dense racemes of pink cups about 15-20cm (6–8in) tall. It flowers best in sun and when congested in a pot looks quite effective. There is also a rare white form in cultivation.

Sternbergia

Although small in terms of number of species, the genus Sternbergia provides one of the reliable highlights of autumn, both in the open garden and under glass. There are probably only eight species, with six of these flowering in autumn. They have yellow funnel-shaped flowers, of varying size and shape.

They are found in the Mediterranean basin and western Asia, growing in alkaline soils which dry out quite radically in summer. They need a sunny position, with most flowering best under glass, where the bulbs can be ripened to ensure bud formation. The flowers are very weather-tolerant and last well once open.

Sternbergia clusiana

This bulb, uncommon in cultivation, is from the eastern end of the Mediterranean, reaching as far as Iran in distribution. A large-flowered species, it needs a big pot or a bulb frame to grow well. The substantial bulbs produce a large root mass, which needs more space than immediately obvious to grow well. The flowers come before the leaves and are substantial, upward-facing yellow goblets, which open quite widely. The leaves follow much later in winter and spring.

Sternbergia colchiciflora

This is the smallest sternbergia species. The yellow, upright, slim trumpets are 2–3cm (¾–1¼in) long and borne at ground level, in mid autumn. The dark green, slightly twisted linear leaves follow in winter. This is definitely a plant for pot culture and then on a bench where the flowers are close to the eye. Accidentally I top-dressed a bed beneath a fastigate oak tree with seed from this plant, which after a few years duly flowered following a wet August. It looked really quite effective, but tiny, revelling in the dry conditions provided by the tree. It is an easily cultivated little bulb that regularly sets seed.

Sternbergia greuteriana

A species with a very limited distribution, found only on Crete and the island of

Karpathos. It looks like a smaller form of *Sternbergia sicula*, but has a longer stem, which raises the flowers above the leaves. It can easily be grown in a pot under cold glass.

Sternbergia lutea

The most widely grown sternbergia, *Sternbergia lutea* is of strong constitution, simply requiring a sunny site to flower well right through autumn. The yellow goblets vary in size, from 3–5cm (1¼–2in) in length, with the width of each segment giving extra substance to some of the flowers. In cool temperate climates in all but the hottest summers the leaves tend to show just before flowers emerge and can elongate, masking the display. The leaves are glossy green, slightly channelled and usually over 5mm (¼in) wide. In the Mediterranean basin, where the plant is often found in olive groves, the flowers appear before the leaves. There is some variation in colour, from a true yellow to a primrose yellow, and very occasionally a double-flowered form when large colonies are explored.

Below: *Sternbergia lutea*

Sternbergia pulchella

A rare species from Syria and the Lebanon. It flowers in early autumn and is preceded by the quite broad keeled leaves, which lengthen considerably as winter approaches. The flowers are bright yellow, held on short stems and barely 2cm (¾in) long. It seems to be easily grown under cold glass.

Sternbergia sicula

A very choice bulb to grow under glass. It will survive outside, but is very much better under glass. There is some confusion in naming plants that have broader than average

Below *Sternbergia lutea.*
Right: *Sternbergia lutea* (double-flowered form)

leaves, which could be classified as *Sternbergia lutea* if leaf width were the only criterion. However, when grown in full light, the flowers have shorter and slimmer stems than their cousins and there is a certain jizz that defines them. The most attractive forms of *Sternbergia sicula* have narrow, dark green leaves with a thin silver line down the centre and deep yellow, chalice-like flowers which are held close to the ground. There are many named forms available, so it is best to buy them in flower.

The leaves are beginning to grow at flowering but tend to spread to frame the flowers rather than competing for space with them. If pot-grown they do need a deep root run or better still, the freedom provided by a bulb frame.

Tigridia

A brightly flowered bulbous plant from Mexico and Central America. Generally tender, but easily stored through winter in a dry, frost-free place. In spring the bulbs can be planted out in a sunny spot to flower in late summer through to September. They are quick to flower from seed (two to three years) sown in spring when the chance of frost has diminished.

The bulbs are covered in a coarse tunic and are best planted out some 10cm (4in) deep in a sunny, well-drained position as the frost risk lessens. They require ample moisture throughout the growing season and respond well to liquid feeding.

Tigridia multiflora
A Mexican species, 40cm (16in) tall with brown-orange or purple upward-facing flowers some 4cm (1½in) across.

Tigridia pavonia
The most widely grown plant, with many colour forms, each with its own name. The flowers have two very distinct sets of segments. The outer three very colourful ones form a cup and then spread out to form a triangle, which can reach 10cm (4in) in diameter. The inner three are much smaller and have a definite waist. The outer segments of the type are orange-scarlet, with a ring of spotted deep crimson near the base. Selections can be orange, yellow, white and colours in between. Each of these flowers lasts for a day, but a succession is produced for many weeks. The plant reaches 45–60cm (18–24in) and has sparse sword-like foliage attached to the stem.

Zephyranthes

These attractive bulbs have upward-facing, trumpet-shaped flowers of clear colours ranging from white (sometimes tinged with green) and pink to yellow. The stamens are always the same length. They have quite sparse, strap-shaped leaves, which are produced before and during flowering.

They are commonly called the 'rain lilies', for their ability to flower quite quickly after the onset of rain. In the garden this is most obvious in one of the hardier species, *Zephyranthes candida*, which flowers within a few weeks of a late summer rainstorm. For the majority, in pots or the frame, the flowering can be reasonably timed by the judicious use of the watering can.

This genus is composed of about thirty or so species, all from the south-eastern USA, Central and South America. The flowering times vary, but there are a significant number that flower in early to mid-autumn. They are strangely neglected, probably because they do not fit into the usual regime of watering and the time of potting. If the bulbs are received in late summer they may not begin rooting until next spring, which if over-watered can lead to some losses. The best practice is to pot on and divide in late winter, or spring in the open garden. They

Opposite: *Tigridia pavonia* (Chrysalis Image Library)

thrive in freely drained conditions and, like many bulbs, seem to flower better if quite pot-bound. The perfect recipe for lazy gardening! However, this species does appreciate feeding, so some liquid feed provided during the growing season promotes strong growth and flowering. They set copious seed, which hangs in the capsule inviting collection for weeks and is best sown in spring for a swift germination.

Zephyranthes atamasco

This species is from the swampy woodland of the south-eastern USA. A large-flowered bulb with white-tinged-with-pink trumpets some 8cm (3¼in) in diameter, held on 30cm (12in) stems. Not hardy, but easily grown in a cool greenhouse.

Zephyranthes candida

This species produces a beautiful white crocus-like flower, sometimes with a touch of pink towards the base, in September and October. The trumpets are about 5cm (2in) long and held on 20cm (8in) stems. The rush-like foliage is almost evergreen and in a sheltered position this can be a very effective garden bulb. Otherwise, pot cultivation suits well, as long as the quite large fleshy roots are accommodated. The bulb comes from the low-lying areas around the La Plata river between Uruguay and Argentina, making it one of the most southerly species.

Zephyranthes citrina

As its name suggests, this plant has yellow flowers, some 5cm (2in) long with a green base. The rush-like leaves are there at flowering. Definitely a bulb for the greenhouse, but worth the effort as it is very distinct and attractive.

Zephyranthes flavissima

A South American species of quite small stature, with narrow green leaves and yellow funnel-shaped flowers up to 3cm (1¼in) long. A relatively new introduction, which seems to be worth trying in a sheltered position when stocks permit.

Zephyranthes grandiflora

One of the finest species, with stems to 30cm (12in), topped by 7cm (3in) long, slightly upward-facing pink trumpets. Although coming from Mexico and neighbouring countries it is surprisingly hardy and has survived and flowered outside in some favoured parts of the UK. Best in a pot in a free-draining compost and then only repotted when very congested. It sometimes flowers before the leaves, generally in late summer or early autumn.

Zephyranthes rosea

Native to Guatemala, this species should be very tender, but is proving to withstand some frost, as long as the drainage is good. The narrow strap-like leaves are produced at flowering in late summer into early autumn. The flowers are 3cm (1¼in) long, pink with a greenish base.

Opposite: *Zephyranthes candida*

EXPLORING AUTUMN BULBS IN THE MEDITERRANEAN

In the Mediterranean the climate condenses the growing season for small plants into about two-thirds of the year. As an adaptation to this reduction, some bulbs flower in autumn, thus taking advantage of an equable month or so to ensure pollination by the insects of summer which are still much in evidence. The leaves often begin to grow as the flowers fade and then last through winter and well into spring. These flowering highlights in October and November are very welcome and provide opportunities for flower holidays in the northern hemisphere. Areas bordering the Mediterranean basin all have significant floral displays at this time of year, but a few are just that little bit more diverse and are therefore more favoured by visitors to the region.

Greece has an amazing bulbous flora, without equal in autumn. The proximity of the Greek peninsula to the migration of European flora from the north and Asian flora from the east, plus the peripheral Mediterranean flora, has led to a great diversity of over 6000 plants, with a number of endemics. The area was little affected by the recent ice age. However, there is always significant snow cover on the higher mountains well into summer. This snow-melt moisture is an important element in the survival of some bulbous plants, providing abundant moisture in spring and even into early summer, just when it is needed most.

Much of Greece is limestone, often metamorphosed to such an extent that the usual layers are completely distorted. Generally the red terra-rossa soils overlie the limestone and, although lacking in humus, they are rich in minerals and support the greatest range of plants. The older, crystalline rocks, which are usually acidic, produce soils that are poorer in nutrients and certainly less interesting florally. Greece's limestone mountains have been sculpted into many isolated peaks, often separated by deep gorges, all elements that help to reinforce the containment of endemic species and the evolution of new ones. In particular, the Peloponnese is rich in autumn flowers, with crocus taking centre stage. The Taygetos and Parnon mountain ranges and the surrounding plains provide a feast of crocus, colchicums, cyclamen, sternbergias, narcissus and even the odd anemone. Further north and east on the mainland and on the islands there are more discoveries awaiting, but not in the high density of further south.

The larger islands of Crete and Cyprus have interesting autumn highlights. Crete generally peaks in late October to early November, whereas in Cyprus the drought of summer takes longer to break down and mid-November sees it at its best. The southern coast and mountain hinterland of southern Turkey still retain a Mediterranean climate and are magnets for cyclamen lovers at this season. They can also offer some stunning endemics such as *Sternbergia candida* and *Galanthus peshmenii*. Very widely spread, but worth seeking, are the large-flowered forms of colchicum: *Colchicum cilicium* in the south and the ubiquitous *Colchicum speciosum* in damp meadows in the north-east of Turkey and in the Caucasus. Further west, choice plants are to be found in Italy and the coastal parts of France – *Crocus medius*, *Leucojum autumnale* and *Sternbergia lutea* to name but a few. The Balearic islands are home to the tiny

Crocus cambessedesii and the much larger *Arum pictum*, with its beautifully veined leaves, and the diminutive pink-flowered *Leucojum roseum* is found on Corsica and Sardinia.

More Mediterranean highlights are the autumn-flowering narcissus from the Iberian peninsula and adjacent North Africa. Here the size of the land mass leads to immense changes in climate from the virtually frost-free coasts in the south-west to the truly continental climate of the interior with great temperature ranges, but everywhere is still very dry in summer. There are a number of autumn-flowering species such as *Narcissus papyraceus*, *Narcissus humilis*, *Narcissus serotinus* and *Narcissus viridiflorus* that are distributed in southern Spain and across the straits of Gibraltar in Morocco and Algeria. In Morocco, *Narcissus cantabricus* subsp. *cantabricus* var. *foliosus* can be found in flower as early as October in the mountains of the western Rif and the north-eastern Middle Atlas. The western end of the Mediterranean basin has fewer crocus species, with just *Crocus serotinus* and its varieties having a similar distribution to the narcissus and *Crocus nudiflorus* from south-western France and eastern Spain.

Most of these countries are now connected by low-cost scheduled flights, and some hotels are starting to extend their opening seasons to accommodate bulb-hunting visitors. Temperatures are fairly warm – rather like summer in more temperate regions – and there is often some light rain. A dry autumn, on the other hand, produces spasmodic flowering of short duration. In this case, seek out perennial water-courses and deciduous woodland, particularly on north- and east-facing slopes, where humidity is higher, to improve your chances of finding flowers.

BIBLIOGRAPHY

Bishop, Matthew et al *Snowdrops* (Griffin Press, 2001)

Blanchard, John *Narcissus* (AGS 1990)

Boyce, Peter *The Genus Arum* (HMSO 1993)

Bryan, John E *Bulbs* (Helm 1989)

European Garden Flora Committee, Ed. *The European Garden Flora* (Cambridge University Press 1986)

Grey-Wilson, Christopher *Cyclamen* (Batsford 1997)

Huxley, Anthony and Taylor, William *Flowers of Greece and the Aegean* (Chatto and Windus 1977)

KAVB *International Checklist for Hyacinths and Miscellaneous Bulbs* (1991)

Mathew, Brian *Dwarf Bulbs* (Batsford 1973)

Mathew, Brian *Growing Bulbs* (Batsford 1997)

Mathew, Brian *Larger Bulbs* (Batsford 1978)

Mathew, Brian *The Crocus* (Batsford 1982)

Mathew, Brian *The Smaller Bulbs* (Batsford 1987)

Mathew, Brian *The Garden* Vol 118 part 1 pp36–37 (RHS, 1993)

Nutt, R D *Snowdrop Cultivars and Colchicums in Cultivation* (Journal of the Scottish Rock Garden Club 1971)

Phillips, Roger and Rix, Martyn *Bulbs* (Pan 1981, 1989)

RHS *Plant Finder 2003–2004* (Dorling Kindersley/RHS 2003)

Synge, Patrick *Collins Guide to Bulbs* (Collins 1961, 1971)

Wells, James S *Modern Miniature Daffodils*

INDEX

Page numbers in **bold** refer to illustrations.